THE
DEMOCRACY COVENANT

A Timeless Dream…A Promise Broken…
Democracy's Travail

TABLE OF CONTENTS

PART ONE

DEMOCRACY'S PROMISE

"We hold these truths to be self-evident, that all men are created equal, that they are endowed by their Creator with certain unalienable Rights, that among these are Life, Liberty and the pursuit of happiness—That to secure these rights, Governments are instituted among Men, deriving their just powers from the consent of the governed."

The first sentence, second paragraph, of America's Declaration of Independence proclaims three principles upon which American democracy is founded: that all persons are created equal; that every person is entitled to certain unalienable rights; and that government is instituted to secure those rights. These are the indispensable principles of legitimate government, and the core of democracy's promise: the declaration of human equality and the freedom of every person to pursue their happiness, restrained only by justice, the rights of others, and the common good. It is a promise unfulfilled—the historical longing for human equality betrayed yet again by the unyielding demand of the selfish brain for power and privilege over others. The self-evident truths, **"created equal"** and **"right to life"** imply an *unalienable right to a life of fundamental equality*.

"Let us re-adopt the Declaration of Independence, and with it, the practices, and policy, which harmonize with it." (Abraham Lincoln, Oct. 16, 1854).

American democracy has not secured the unalienable rights of life; it has added civil laws to Hobbes' jungle—**"a condition of war of everyone against everyone"** (*Leviathan*, 1651)—seeking to protect the unequal results of economic and political competition for social dominance against violent redress—civil laws that lessen the violence of the jungle, but not the desperate struggle for livelihood; giving selfish desires for superiority the legitimacy and "freedom" to achieve private economic wealth, and thereby the political power to control democratic government, preventing fulfillment of democracy's promise, and inculcating an acceptance in the public mind that social inequality is good because it results from *free* competition––ignoring the emotional and psychological violence of unrewarded struggle, unrecognized dignity, and unequal security of life. Capitalist democracy achieves outcomes that violate the declared principles of popular democracy—**"of, by, and for, the people."**—by permitting private power achieved through financial wealth to eclipse the democratic power of the sovereign people. *America is not a people's democracy because America is not a people's economy*: a people's economy would minimize wealth inequality—preventing private economic power from becoming political power. In a democracy, the benefits of economic growth must spread outward, not upward. Political democracy will not fulfill its promise without a democratic economy—the elimination of private wealth accumulation that corrupts and subverts public authority and purpose.

Wealth inequality is destroying American democracy: "freedom" is not a legitimate path to tyranny; nor is economic "ownership" a right to political power. Private wealth is not the friend of democracy—the declaration of **"created equal"** is a *covenantal rejection* of all presumptions or systems or laws that create or allow substantial inequality.

"Fascism begins the moment a ruling class, fearing the people may use their political democracy to gain economic democracy, begins to destroy political democracy in order to retain its power of exploitation and special privilege." (Author unknown) (Emphasis added).

The democratic requirement of civil law is that it respects the inalienable rights of life and not be a system of laws and rules that merely legitimate and protect the traditions of inequality that have historically been a usurpation by force.

"That to secure these rights, Governments are instituted among Men, deriving their just powers from the consent of the governed." (Declaration of Independence; 1776).

"Man's capacity for justice makes democracy possible; but man's inclination to injustice makes democracy necessary." (Reinhold Niebuhr; *The Children of Light and The Children of Darkness*, 1944, Forward).

"Oligarchy is when men of property have the government in their hands." (Aristotle: Ethics, Book 3, Part 8).

There is no inalienable right to a private power to obstruct the will of the sovereign people, or a right for private power to control the mediums of information. When a representative body fails to enact the laws that secure the rights of the sovereign people over private power democracy has been subverted.

The term "liberal" is immensely confusing: in economics, it refers to Classical Liberalism—the unregulated free-market economy of Adam Smith's *The Wealth of Nations*, published in 1776. The word "liberal" derives from the Latin word "liber," meaning "free." The philosophy and moral aspirations of liberalism arose from the Enlightenment, the 17th and 18th century escape from centuries of theocratic darkness. As understood politically and morally liberal means human equality and freedom—release from historical systems of imposed inequality—the world of aristocrats and serfs. Thus, liberal moral and political "freedom" contains an implicit limitation: *freedom cannot be a path to new inequalities*, implying the regulation of classical liberal *economic* freedom to prevent unjust inequalities in political and social outcomes; securing a democracy of justice and equality for all. The freedom of liberal *economics* (neoliberalism, unregulated capitalism) is antithetical to the freedom and equal rights of liberal *democracy*. Neoliberalism uses "freedom" to achieve and justify private wealth and class inequality—*a condition of competition of everyone against everyone* to achieve class superiority, protected by government instead of prevented by government. Whereas, America is founded on a declaration of equality, unalienable rights, and the purpose of government to secure these rights, an unregulated private enterprise economy achieves inequality—opulence for a few and insecurity for many—and buys government's support.

Since liberal means individual freedom, almost everyone is a liberal—from far Left to far Right. Who doesn't believe in their personal freedom to pursue happiness? The most elucidating political and social distinction is between *humanitarian* liberal (freedom and well-being for all), and *egocentric* liberal (freedom and well-being, and *opportunity to achieve inequality*, for me and my friends).

In American politics, conservatives are universally economic liberals—opposed to government regulation of the economy to secure unalienable rights—except when the freedom of economic interests ignore conservative traditions and instigate threatening changes to the status quo (Much more on the conservative fear of change below). Democrats are a mix of economic liberalism and social liberalism, uncomfortable with inequality and injustice, and wishing that economic freedom had a stronger and more equitable "invisible hand." *but unwilling to restrain the competitive race to greater inequality.*

Understanding the term "liberal" requires understanding whose freedom to do what. Conscientious members of a democratic community recognize moral limits on their personal freedom. Egocentricity lacks that recognition.

. . . .

A competitive social system does not sufficiently tame the Hobbesian struggle for survival to provide neurological security to the developing brain, resulting in harmful emotional and cognitive impacts upon brain structure and function; often expressed in anti-other attitudes—political and cultural beliefs and behaviors that produce division and discord. Competition for achieving a basic level of well-being and security of life is confining mankind to its primal fears—we hesitate to cooperate because we are too afraid to trust, and too selfish to share, so we remain mired in competition and conflict.

There is a dilemma known as the Hobbesian Trap: it refers to the situation where mutual fear leads to escalating fear and the increased probability of violent conflict. It is the same with selfish competition: selfish acts provoke selfish responses. The greater the genetic level of fear—hyperactive amygdala (ah-MIG-dah-la)—the greater the inclination to selfishness and the expedient abandonment of moral principles. Selfish escalations instill libertarian priorities and erode attention and obligation to the common good; government *for the people* becomes government for the selfish achievers... oligarchy then takes over democracy. Hobbesian escalations continue until one side gains the power to prevail—authoritarianism. Neoliberalism provides the freedom to exert private power over public power— America's emerging socio-political reality.

"Americans must forswear that conception of the acquisition of wealth which, through excessive profits, creates undue private power over...public affairs." (Franklin Roosevelt; *State of the Union*, 1935).

. . . .

The following hypothesis offers a cause for the failed promise: the fearful brain—a brain whose early development is dominated by the emotions of primal fear tends not to acquire an *evolved* sensibility for moral and democratic principles. It will be a brain of intensified self-interest and undeveloped empathy and compassion for others, employing expedient strategies for social advantage in opposition to **"all men are created equal."** We will explore the neuropsychology of the fearful brain, and the implications of "Life" and "Liberty," the pillars of the promise. THE QUESTION: If all persons are **"created equal,"** by what right or necessity, and for whose benefit, are they made unequal in society... by what right is Nature's provision to all, ceded preferentially to a few?

Neuropsychology is the study of the relationship of belief and behavior to brain structure and function. The brain is a biological machine analogous to any machine, its optimal performance and behavioral product depend on all parts—brain regions—working properly in relation to each other. It is proposed here that a hyper-reactive amygdala's response to perceived threat impacts the early brain with excessive fear emotions that suppress or derange the development of moral sentiments and cognitive independence, resulting in *a brain whose **incipient** cognitive faculty is conditioned by the **amygdala's early life neural dominance** into subservience to primal fear emotions* (Freud's id) by rationalizing justifications and expedient strategies for self-advancing behavior—persistent patterns of deceit, hypocrisy, and authoritarian lust for power—rather than providing reasoned restraint and guidance based on truth and ethical principles (superego). Selfish ambitions for dominance then triumph over moral character; sociopolitical tribes become enemies; and the shadow of autocracy looms over democracy. The brain's prefrontal cortex becomes a conservative think tank, not envisioning improvements for the common good, but preferences and advantages for the selfish brain—the desires of the psychopaths and narcissists, and egocentric liberals.

Opposition to human equality results from this failure of the brain's cognitive faculty to develop morally informed control of a hyperactive amygdala's fear generated behavior- - xenophobia, greed, aggression, social/political dominance seeking to prevent the advancement of others. It is a brain that remains oriented to primal defense responses whose exaggerated assessment of threat in the environment results in a wariness and mistrust that incites what it forebodes— interminable human conflict. In the absence of pro-social, empathetic *cognitive* functionality to moderate fear-based *emotions*, both threat avoidance and pleasure seeking become highly egocentric, pursuing dominant and exploitative rather than respectful and egalitarian relationship to others. The fear-based brain eagerly abandons Truth and moral principle for the expediencies of self-interest—lies, hypocrisy, and false accusation to create enemies and scapegoats—manipulation of the public mind in pursuit of economic and political control. Not democracy, but autocracy is the aim of the fear inspired mind, *absolute control to eliminate the threat of democratic change*— improvements for the common good. Fear seeks the power to be fearless, vulnerability the power to be invulnerable, and selfish desires the power to assure gratification.

It is important to recognize that amygdala hyper-sensitivity to threat is not the only developmental pathway to anti-other political and economic selfishness. Other genetic factors and early life experiences, and *cultural/tribal indoctrination*, are also informing of who we become. The early brain is developing in response to genetic instructions and environmental impacts—*brain structure and function are being formed prior to conscious awareness*. We are not choosing ourself, we are being made… a product of the influences that structure our brains and impel our behaviors. Upon birth we are placed on a cultural conveyor belt, a brain assembly line where early experiences in the birth environment initiate the brain's structural responses— adaptation for survival. We are not born into freedom; we are clay to be molded by external circumstances.

It begins in utero: the rapidly developing brain's—100 billion neurons by birth—sensory awareness of the fetal environment begins around 26 weeks after conception, with all senses responding to sensory inputs by the time of birth. Also, at birth the amygdala's fear system is fully functional- -with the amygdala having been functional since the eighth month of gestation; meaning it has begun monitoring sensory inputs for signs of threat in utero, in preparation for the transition to life. Amygdala responsiveness implies that birth from fetal to infant environment is likely experienced by the newborn's fear system as an alarming change of circumstance… the first awakening of the survival instinct.

The change from gestation to birth involves major physical alterations: air and breathing replace lung fluid, temperature drops from warmth to cold, darkness turns to bright light, quiet and the maternal voice are replaced by strange sounds and unfamiliar voices, feeding reroutes from the maternal bloodstream to objects entering mouth, physical pressure on the scull from passage through the birth canal, suspension in a fluid repose transformed to physical handling—and perhaps most critically, removal from the mother's cradle, from symbiotic connection into the shock of separation—the vulnerability of aloneness. Drastic *environmental change* becomes the amygdala's introduction to the perils of living—the anticipation that life entails threats to life. The immediate necessity is for some comforting reconnection with the maternal environment—the mother's bodily warmth, her emotional rhythms, and the sound of her assuring voice—to minimize the trauma of separation; and thus, *the level of amygdala reactivity to its perceived fears*.

At birth the amygdala's journey has only begun—now cultural conditioning begins; the cultural conveyor belt rolls, feeding local experiences and influences into the amygdala's fear system (limbic system), building synaptic circuits that form fear-sensitive interpretations of sensory information into programmed beliefs and behaviors and memories—and political affiliations—that mollify the emotions of fear. Conformation to surrounding conditions is another phrase for adaptation for survival. Defense of a received environment then becomes the primary motive in the opposition to changes in the environment as a threat to the survival instinct.

We are all egocentric in matters of survival, in matters of achieving and defending our protective and comforting habitats. When change threatens our sense of security defensiveness becomes defense of life. The test that human initiated change must meet is maximizing good and minimizing bad effects for most people—removing the wrongs that overly benefit some at the cost of deprivation to others. There will never be an arrangement of circumstances that please everyone, only the possibility of an equilibrium that does not offend the morality of fairness to all. In the bigger reality, change is inevitable, a constant current, an unstoppable wave of motion through time that the elements of existence demand.

The amygdala is unimpeded: the cognitive brain's (prefrontal cortex) ability to reason and ascertain facts, does not emerge until age 7, only then beginning to evaluate and moderate the amygdala's assessment of reality; giving the brain an alternative path for relating to life with less fear. Even infant self-consciousness does not begin to emerge until sometime in the first year of life, leaving the amygdala the sole unobserved architect of the brain's formation.

But in many cases, the cognitive brain has already been compromised by the amygdala's 7 years of early neural dominance into a mercenary on the side of liberal egocentricity—a warrior against change, against the humanitarian's quest for the well-being of all people.

. . . .

The first imperative for all living things is physical survival. The second imperative is truth about the environment in which life is struggling to survive—successful adaptation requires knowledge of what is true of the physical and social habitat. The third imperative is brain plasticity, being able to learn and thus knowingly and willingly adapt—the neural flexibility to modify formerly conditioned belief and behavior based on new information. A flexible brain allows facts to alter beliefs; a rigid brain denies facts to preserve beliefs. In the fear-based brain emotion supersedes reason, suppressing brain plasticity: reassuring beliefs appease emotional fears—and they need not be based on truth or reason. A fourth imperative is the ability to distinguish between acceptable and unacceptable change in the environment—the political war between humanitarian progress and egocentric resistance. Escaping the Hobbesian Trap requires human brains that can transcend their amygdala fears.

Evolution has selected both selfish and benevolent traits; both have aided human survival. Primal fear is initially selfish; it is the brain's instinctual reflex to the perception of imminent danger in the environment; the individual is instantly prepared to run or fight to defend his survival, and the habitat to which he has adapted. But as we have just described, the degree of amygdala reaction to birth trauma will determine the level of fear that will dictate the brain's structural response—the formation of synaptic circuits that pave the path to humanitarian liberal or egocentric liberal... the guidance of moral principle or the permissions of expedient rationalizations.

As some individuals learned there was greater safety in groups, sociable and cooperative traits were selected, allowing a rational path to survival. But that did not result in lessening the more reactive amygdala's fear—the more primitive, lingering emotions of the fearful brain remain in political conflict with the evolved emotions of sympathy with others—*the conservative reactive opposition to social liberal ideas of justice and equality.* The selfish pursuit of social superiority as an escape from primal fear disregards the rights of others—the desire for advantage and superiority denies The Declaration's assertion of natural equality, and minimizes the mutual benefits and obligations of cooperative community. The individual interest versus the common interest is man's ongoing predicament; he is trapped on a selfish-selfless spectrum, and mired in the politics of antagonism between the humanitarian principles of democracy, and the selfish brain's authoritarian pursuit of dominance. A government of the people cannot be for the people when the people are not for each other.

"Selfish and contentious people will not cohere, and without coherence nothing can be effected." (Charles Darwin, *The Descent of Man*, 1871).

Genetic inheritance, personal experiences, education, intensity of cultural indoctrination (belief and ideology); *and critically*, the security and affection of the parental environment, especially the emotional and physical closeness of the mother, determine *the experiential conditions that will form the developing brain.* Whether our infant brain experiences the birth environment as comforting or discomforting will set the stage for our performance in life. The first five years of brain development places us on the amygdala scale: sacrifice of humane associations to the immediacies of primal fear, or freed to find the possibilities of moral principle and a benevolent rationality unshackled from the amygdala's alarm.

"The human genome containing around 20,000...genes can provide the basic blueprint for brain development, but training and experiences in the early years from infancy through childhood are crucially important in sculpting brain development and function...prosocial behavior is displayed by most infants and preschool children...societies that tend to focus on individual achievement and "success" result in children that are less prosocial and that exhibit fewer altruistic tendencies...Culture has more than one order of magnitude greater influence than genes on altruism and prosocial behavior." (Front. Psychology; 2018; 9: 575).

The postnatal brain needs immediate assurance that its new surroundings are not only safe, but supportive and caring, and beaming with the radiance of loving acceptance. For what we do not receive we do have; and what we do not have we cannot give.

. . . .

The neoliberal competition for even a minimal security of life not only precludes the realization of democratic principles and promises, it restrains human character from continuing the long climb out of its primitive origins. Competitive vigor scorns the equitable aspirations of decency.

It is difficult to gain the moral sensibilities we leave childhood without. Genetic inheritance and early experience impose a brain structure and function that will determine what we believe and how we behave, and it is not easily reversed—for the survival imperative requires the brain to learn about and adapt to the environment, to become what we must to survive. And then to imprint through repetition the beliefs and behaviors that have *appeared* to relieve our fears and aided our survival. *The brain that does not develop critical cognitive independence and flexibility will be anchored to its initial orientations.* The importance of education lies in expanding the formative environment to challenge the impressions of our first experiences. *"Freedom" may be more about escaping who we became, than unhindered performance of who we were made to be.* Education, as well, is the best means of escaping the lies and intentions of authoritarians.

Childhood is a process of learning, of finding one's way to live successfully in the social environment in which one has been placed. Once success is comfortably achieved—and for many it never is—the brain becomes dependent, to a greater or lesser degree, on the maintenance of that environment... hence, one's personal politics—liberal openness and desire for social improvements suggests less dependency on existing conditions, and a moral sensibility for their inadequacy. The conservative reaction to the liberal's pursuit of improvements implies a deep primal sense of threat to his familiar and protective environment. Political and violent conflicts are between the defense of what was and what is, and the aspiration for what should be.

(In this text when "liberal" is used without an adjective such as classical or neo or egocentric, it refers to the moral sensibility and a respect for equality and justice for all.)

Even 2000 years of Christianity, which professes to teach love, forgiveness, mercy, and kindness to strangers, and gives warnings to sinners of eternal damnation, has not moderated sufficiently the fear emotions that breed conflict and mayhem to achieve **"peace on earth, and goodwill toward men"**—despite the promise of eternal salvation.

"Faith alone," are the words that eviscerated the teaching of **"do unto others as you would have them do unto you."** "Works" must be done; "faith" only avowed. Why bear the conscience of Christ when faithful appearance allows you to merely pretend it? The amygdala brain's golden rule is: "do unto others before they do unto you." Conservative "dirty tricks."

....

Neoliberalism's free-market ideology makes the security of life a competitive rather than cooperative enterprise; and its reward in wealth and power for competitive success systematically reinforces the aggressively selfish brain and disadvantages the less aggressive, prosocial brain. Left unregulated, neoliberalism produces social and political inequality, thereby undermining the principles and promises of democracy. Neoliberalism does not secure equal rights for all **("government is instituted to secure these rights")**, it gives freedom for the individual's disregard of equal rights: *"equal opportunity" is not a sufficient recognition of equal rights*. A culture that induces selfish behavior through economic competition for wealth and power—or mere survival—is a progenitor of sociopathy; it does not select virtue; it selects the compromises of virtue that achieve advantage... the various expedient modes of "success." The neoliberal embrace of unregulated economic activity gives leeway to the corruptibility of fear-based self-interest—the neurological absence of an ethical conscience.

There is a great irony in Classical Liberalism's journey: it emerged in opposition to the inherited power and privilege of traditional aristocracy. It believed that equal rights and free-market competition among free individuals would arrive at a just and secure society for all. Thus, it began as a force against traditional inequality that has produced its own inequality that now threatens democracy. The fascistic insistence on dominance destroys political democracy to prevent the people from using it to achieve economic democracy. *Neoliberalism means neo-inequality.*

Friedrich Hayek's famed "spontaneous order" description of neoliberal free-market economics is a scramble of greed and deception where all the seven deadly sins are given freedom alongside the virtues of modesty and good faith, resulting in a social hierarchy replete at the top with diminished human character. *Neoliberalism is the practice that repeals democracy's promise.*

Evolution's defect is the excessive fear response of a hyper-reactive amygdala—a descendant of prey animals living in trees to avoid predators—driving a selfish, xenophobic and competitive individualism that seeks the power to dominate its fears, obstructing the realization of a benevolent community. There is perhaps a no more vicious creature than a former prey animal that gains the power to become the apex predator; an evolutionary victim of predation with the power to lay vengeance upon its fears.

Evolution may have given the human brain too much intelligence too rapidly: the ability to discover and conceive, and accumulate knowledge of the environment, provides an opportunity for improvement and change that the primal brain's fear cannot abide. Instead, fear seeks to enlist the complicity of that evolving intelligence. For then, it could not only fight or flee more successfully, it would be able to plot and strategize for political control of the community and forestall progress toward the greater good (conservative reaction). Reason can serve to oppress or liberate.

Thus, humanity's fate lies in whether intelligence embraces morality and moderates the amygdala's fear to find human kinship, or conspires with fear to insist on the continuance of selfishness, injustice, corruptibility, and partisan warfare.

"The more recently evolved components of the nervous system depend on the function of more ancient systems. Neocortical structures are in general subservient to systems necessary for survival. More primitive systems and behaviors, including those associated with fear and anxiety, may inhibit positive social behaviors and cognitive strategies." (NIMH: Social Neuroscience and Behavior: From Basic to Clinical Science, 4/14/2006).

The basic point of this hypothesis is that the "evolved" regions of the human brain (reason and moral principle) remain largely subservient to the primitive regions (emotional reaction to threat) for a great part of humanity. We are in an evolutionary moment of struggle between the persisting sins of fear (id) and the aspiring virtues of reason (superego), displayed in the ideology and politics of Right and Left—the brain in servitude to primal fears opposing the brain evolving toward principle and reason and promising possibilities. Humanity is divided between two brain states: moral rationality and selfish expedience. *There is in this moment of human evolution a great need for an accelerated natural selection of moral rationality.*

We experience the world emotionally before we understand it rationally; excessive fear emotions, reinforced by prejudiced cultural indoctrination, shape childhood brain development toward fear-driven responses to sensory experiences perceived as threatening, precluding the development of a moral and altruistic and reasoned response to experience—objective facts give way to beliefs that mollify alarmed emotions. When truth threatens, or is unknown, the untruth and the imagined truth become salvation. The conservative invokes "free speech" to propagate lies, then invents "wokeness" to vilify truth. In both cases the motive is to conceal its own character—we don't want the truths that defame us, we want lies that defame the truth. *People accept the lie because it offers the reality they want.*

The words of The Declaration make it clear that America was founded on the political principles of natural equality and the right to life, not an economic design rewarding behavior that subverts those principles—subordinating the principle of equality to an economic system based on an opportunity to achieve inequality; making "freedom" the enemy of **"created equal."** Thus, whatever **"the pursuit of happiness"** means, it does not mean the freedom to circumvent the rights of life and equality. To embrace a principle and ignore or evade or impede its evident implications is to betray that principle:

"Forms grow out of principles, and operate to continue the principles they grow from...wherever the forms in any government are bad, it is a certain indication that the principles are bad also." (Thomas Paine, *Rights of Man*, 1791).

"...the true system...of political philosophy...was to supply, not a set of model institutions, but principles from which the institutions suitable to any given circumstances might be deduced."
(J.S. Mill; *Autobiography*, 1873).

The American government is bound by a founding covenant to institute the social forms that **"secure these rights."** From the laws of Nature—the biological and environmental facts of life's emergence—derive the **"unalienable Rights"** of Life (yet to be fully deduced); and then also the civil laws and social institutions that serve and secure those rights; *from Natural Law follows Natural Community*. And, therefore, any civil laws and institutions that abridge the common rights of life are a betrayal of the laws of nature and the democratic covenant.

The first purpose, then, of democratic government is to establish institutions that protect the equal security of its citizens, and not institutions that allow an eventual subversion of that equal security in the name of "freedom of opportunity." *Democracy is not a promise to replace titled aristocracy with financial aristocracy.*

All democratic governments derive authority from the sovereign people for the purpose of *securing* their lives and liberties against unjust encroachments. The authority of democratic government is a conditional and amendable convention, established among equal individuals by mutual consent for their mutual protection and benefit. The government satisfies its trust only as its laws and policies realize the principles upon which the government is founded. Every government official, at whatever level, is an employee of the sovereign people—a fact of which presumption should be made aware. Prevailing inequality is not an acceptable outcome to mutual consent and benefit— *a **"certain indication"** that the principles of democracy's promise have been betrayed by the presumptions of neoliberalism.*

....

"Liberty" is herein defined as the protection of individual rights, natural and civil, against the actions of government, the will of a political majority, and the actions of private individuals and organizations. *Liberty is not about what the individual is free to do, it is about the protection of the individual's rights from the actions of others*; government secures the equal rights of each person by prohibiting the infringing actions of others... *the liberty of each limits the freedom of all.* The ideal of freedom as the latitude for individuals to enjoy and direct their lives as they desire—the **"pursuit of happiness"**—does not extend to a right to disregard or subordinate the rights of other individuals, or to acquire the private wealth and power to control a democratic government, *or a right of freedom from economic and financial regulation for democratic purposes by that government.* What each person is due by natural right and equal creation has precedence over what any other person may achieve in the name of personal freedom to pursue happiness. It is liberty, the guarantee of human rights, that makes freedom truly free.

There is no higher human aspiration than the freedom to do good; and none lower than the freedom to do evil. Thus, freedom is not an inalienable right, nor is it a moral principle. It is a conditional latitude that enables the doing of both good and evil, *requiring its restriction to the doing of good, or the doing of nothing.*

Happiness is a subjective state of mind—and sometimes a psychologically deranged state of mind—that cannot be guaranteed satisfaction; self-satisfaction can never be rightly pursued in a manner, or toward ends that impose inequality or harm on the life and liberty of others. In a democracy, there is no right to an individual pursuit of happiness that is injurious to the common good; the outcome of private actions must not violate the principle of equal rights.

"Neoliberalism" is a denial of this principle—it rejects economic security for all, *embracing the rightness of human inequality and social hierarchy*; achieved through a competitive system that allows, and presumes to justify, the "freedom" to gain economic advantage; and thereby, the wealth and power to avert democratic equality. The primary assertion underlying unregulated private enterprise is: *all unequal outcomes are acceptable because they result from individual freedom*. It is notable in American politics that neoliberals rage against proposals for government regulation of the private economy for the common good, but not against lobbying for government policies that protect and further the powers and advantages of private interests. Hypocrisy is the unavoidable recourse for the expedient brain.

Neoliberalism is a 20th century reassertion of Adam Smith's 18th century laissez faire *Classical Liberalism*. It is a reaction of the conservative brain to democratic government's attempt **"to secure these rights"** for all by limiting inequality through regulatory interventions into the private economy. Neoliberalism *frees* the selfish personality from obligation to democratic equality. The sin of selfishness is the presumption of superiority and the merit of privilege; the sin of those who abide the presumption is failure to defend the principles of democracy, and the equal rights of themselves and their children. The elites provide the spectacle of "success;" the multitude provide the admiration and worship of celebrity... to their own disadvantage.

"...and the wondering cheated multitude worshipped the invention." (Thomas Paine; *Rights of Man*, March 16, 1791).

. . . .

In a democracy there are no social outcomes that are beyond the jurisdiction of the common good—**"That to secure these rights, Governments are instituted among Men."** Individual freedom is not an immunity from obligation to the founding covenant; the principle of equality does not mean "equal opportunity" to become unequal.

Freedom—the **"pursuit of happiness"** —is a natural, but not an unalienable right. A degree of personal freedom is one among the several rights that constitute liberty: first is the equal right to life, then the equal protection (liberty) of the natural rights of life, then the right to a freedom of individual action that conforms to the equal rights of others. *Freedom can harm; liberty protects against the freedoms that harm*—violent actions, misinforming speech; the wielding of wealth and power to procure and defend advantage.

The claim for freedom must always be questioned: *whose freedom; freedom to do what; and what is the likely outcome of that freedom on the rights of others?* Neoliberalism is loaded with systemic permissions—laws and rules—that facilitate and obscure the corruption of democratic principles... the laws and institutions that reward avarice and advance human inequality. *Unrestrained freedom is not so valuable that it requires the tolerance of evil.*

Equality is the first declared self-evident truth, it must therefore be presumed to permeate the Constitution as a founding imperative, *even when not explicit*; thus any legislative enactment or judicial interpretation that permits the unequal representation or unequal protection of any individual or group of individuals is a violation of the Constitution and the Declaration of Independence... the founding proclamation of national purpose for securing the natural and equal rights of every citizen. There can be no right, ostensibly justified by a first principle that is exercised in a manner that contradicts the principle; there is no democratic right or freedom to undermine democracy. *Any judicial ruling that upholds a state of unequal representation or unequal protection is on its face unconstitutional, un-American, and anti-democracy.*

Freedom, then, is not a license to establish individual or class inequality; individual ambitions do not supersede democratic principles. The highest human good is the well-being of every individual, not the unequal privilege of a few. A child confined to poverty has more natural right to a better life—and the early life conditions that optimize her brain development to fulfill her possibilities—than the already privileged have to perpetuated or increased overabundance. Selfishness that does not care about the deprivation of others is a resignation from a humane humanity—and a society that is willing to abide the hardship and under development of many for the luxury of a few is neither a good nor a democratic society.

To publicly uphold the ideal of equality, and privately practice the pursuit of inequality, is to hide a malevolent purpose with a false pretense... a common posture among those who only pretend to democratic values. The selfish brain, devoid of guiding values and principles, is ever striving to circumvent democracy; it is the fear-formed brain needing dominance for emotional security and ego-satisfaction.

The necessary conditions of a consensual society are mutual security, mutual benefit, and equality in the essential elements of life's preservation and development. When mutuality and equity are breached consent and legitimacy are forfeited. The highest power in a democracy is not the authority of government; it is the authority of the collection of sovereign individuals acting under, and subservient to, the procedures and principles of democracy, restrained by the rights of minorities.

"That whenever any Form of Government becomes destructive of these ends, it is the Right of the People to alter or abolish it, and to institute new Government, laying its foundation on such principles and organizing its powers in such form, as to them shall seem most likely to effect their Safety and Happiness." (Declaration of Independence, 1776).

. . . .

The critical distinction between *freedom* and *liberty* is a primary premise to this argument: the synonymous use of the terms has allowed an exaggerated focus on individual freedom over the security of equal rights for all, serving an ideological purpose to obscure *the rightful limitations on individual freedom.*

"The world has never had a good definition of the word liberty, and the American people, just now, are much in want of one. We all declare for liberty, but in using the same word we do not all mean the same thing...The shepherd drives the wolf from the sheep's throat, for which the sheep thanks the shepherd as a liberator, while the wolf denounces him for the same act, as the destroyer of liberty...Plainly, the sheep and the wolf are not agreed upon a definition of the word liberty...Here are two, not only different, but *incompatible things*, called by the same name, liberty..." (Abraham Lincoln; Baltimore, April 18, 1864) (Emphasis added).

Nobel laureate F.A. Hayek, in his book, *The Constitution of Liberty*; 1960, quotes the above passage from President Lincoln. Then he writes:

"We are concerned in this book with that condition of men in which coercion of some by others is reduced as much as possible in society. This state we shall describe throughout as a state of liberty or freedom. These two words have also been used to describe many other good things in life. It would therefore not be very profitable to start by asking what they really mean." (Part 1, Chap, 1).

Then in a note to this passage Hayek writes:

"There does not seem to exist any accepted distinction in meaning between the words 'freedom' and 'liberty,' and we shall use them interchangeably." (ibid.)

So, Hayek will write a book employing two of the most important concepts in political philosophy without **"asking**

what they really mean." And since there is no accepted distinction in their meaning, he will continue the confusion. Would not a Nobel Prize winner in economics have sought to define his most cherished terms, and propose a meaningful distinction, at least for the sake of better clarity to his own argument? Hayek quoted Lincoln's passage, so he was cognizant of the distinction. Was there purpose to the synonymous use of the terms? Why would it not be **"profitable"** to make the distinction? *Was there profit in the non-distinction?* Hayek's contribution of the concept of "spontaneous order" did not distinguish between good and bad intentions in human behavior. All were to be free, and the result justified. Hayek was arguing against central government planning, he was not seeking a path to a moral society. The consideration of violated human rights in the scramble for success was not his purview. Throw a handful of marbles in the air and they will all bounce and roll and come to rest in a spontaneous order; pick them up and throw them again and they will find a different spontaneous order. Such "order" is happenstance by the method of chaos. It would not be profitable for thoughts of injustice to complicate his economic argument.

"...the fact that the promises which a free society has to offer can always be only chances and not certainties, only opportunities and not definite gifts..." (F. A. Hayek; *The Constitution of Liberty*, 1960, Chap. 4).

Hayek makes the above statement in the context of asserting that *freedom* is the **"supreme principle;"** that social **"promises"** can only be conditional, otherwise *freedom* will be compromised and slowly eroded. So, the unalienable rights of life and the self-evident truths of The

Declaration, and the Constitution's enumeration of civil rights are only *conditional promises*, to be realized only upon the satisfaction of "freedom." Whose freedom, and freedom to do what is Hayek advocating? The freedom of private interests to subvert the democratic will of the sovereign people? Clearly, Hayek could not promise that spontaneous order would achieve a good outcome, so he had to assert that unalienable rights were also not promises. *Liberty* is not a gift; it is the legitimizing principle and purpose of democratic government: *Liberty is the supreme principle; freedom is a right until it is improperly used.*

Without ascribing motive to Hayek, the confusion allows for an *emphasis on freedom while obscuring the priority of liberty*; that liberty is constituted of those rights, civil and natural, which are guaranteed to all members of a community, and which cannot be rightfully abridged by anyone's freedom to do as they want, whether it be a government, a corporation, or other individuals. Clearly, the consequence of obscuring liberty is to conceal the role of government in securing equal rights; government can then be attacked as the enemy of freedom (**"Government is the problem"**). Without government regulation, the freedom of the wolf prevails—the cherished desire of the selfish brain. The perpetrators of injustice want freedom; the subjugated want liberty… the wolf is not interested in protecting the sheep's liberty. A distinction is *not profitable* when it removes the opportunity to dissemble that is provided by confusion. And democratic regulation of economic outcomes for the common good is not central planning, it is a founding imperative for a government of, by, and for the people.

The *political* liberalism that emerged from The Enlightenment embraced *freedom* and *equality*, culminating in America's democratic revolution. In *apparent harmony*, classical liberalism (unregulated free markets) argued for the freedom of economic activity with no attention to social equality; except for the assurances of "equal opportunity" and "invisible hands" and "unintended consequences." The freedom of the human wolf to be rich and powerful and dominant required disregard for democracy's promise of equal rights and liberty for the sheep. It is the priority of equality that constrains freedom into compatibility with democracy… and makes the conservative brain opposed to democratic progress, and enchanted by authoritarian dreams. Human liberty depends on the restraint of anti-democratic freedoms; Good struggles in this world because Evil is so free.

Mr. Lincoln was right, freedom and liberty **"are two, not only different, but incompatible things, called by the same name."** Hayek will **"use them interchangeably."**

(I cannot refrain from noting that Hayek—in the postscript to "*Why I am not a conservative*"—was concerned to distinguish his views on "liberty" from American conservatism. He writes: **"There is danger in the confused condition...It is therefore important to distinguish clearly the position taken here from that which has long been known...as conservatism."** Sometimes, I guess, distinctions are profitable—as when the intent is to reveal rather than conceal).

. . . .

From the beginning of the classical liberal argument

for economic freedom (Adam Smith's *The Wealth of Nations,* 1776), there was a conflict between freedom and liberty—if the freedom to achieve economic and social inequality was to be justified, it would require the obfuscation of liberty as the protection of an equal right to the fruits of nature... thus the assumption: *if freedom is good and inequality is a consequence, then inequality is good... the means justifies the end.* The right to fundamental equality in the circumstances of life is removed by making liberty just another word for freedom... a thing without a name disappears.

The emerging commercial class of Adam Smith's time was not concerned with protections for the natural rights of serfs. And so, equality of rights was obscured by equality of "opportunity"... a chance to *compete* for equal rights, which meant exposure to the loss of equal rights... *opportunity* removes the *right* to equality. Had liberty as the protection of equal rights been a distinct notion its violation would have been evident... and *an unacceptable consequence invalidates the cause*—opportunity that created inequality would be delegitimized. So, Adam Smith introduced a conjecture disguised as an assurance: that an **"invisible hand"** and **"unintended consequences"** would minimize the violations of equality that the advocates of economic freedom intended. The implication of **"created equal"** as the first self-evident truth is not about opportunity, but *equity in economic condition and civil status.*

Any system or operation or function that relies on unintended consequences for an acceptable outcome is inherently deceptive; and persists only through social inertia and general moral vacuity—and the special interests and true intentions of its agents.

The threat to everyone's liberty and equality is the selfish assumption of individuals to an *unregulated freedom to gain wealth and power over others*. Liberty, as here understood, is the right not to be subjected to the predatory desire of the selfish brain for social dominance. Justice is the prevention of undemocratic dominance, not an equal opportunity to achieve it. The hope for democratic equality has fallen to a wealth aristocracy because avarice was "free" to achieve it. The whole of human political history is a story of aspirations for liberty fighting against *the freedom of selfish ambitions to achieve anti-democratic ends*. In the absence of liberty, freedom means little more than an unhindered struggle to survive... the freedom of gladiators.

. . . .

Government does not create natural rights; government is created by people with natural rights who wish to have their rights secured.

Natural rights derive from the facts of biological creation—life's emergence, and nature's provision of the material conditions for survival... allowing for the evolution of life's innate possibilities. All beings created in nature are naturally free and rightfully *entitled* to access the natural materials and conditions which support their continuing to exist... none being created with a greater natural right to sustenance than another. *Natural entitlement is the basis of natural rights.* What is due by natural right is **"unalienable"** and not subject to loss by the actions of others; the tree that nature grows makes fruit for all, and not for anyone to gain power over others by exclusive possession and denial. The purpose of government is **"to secure these rights"** by instituting the social forms and laws that preserve natural entitlement in society. Any system of competition or notion of private property that disregards, denies, impedes, or fails to protect natural entitlement is a violation of natural law and democracy's covenant.

"I now looked upon the choice of political institutions as a moral question more than one of material interests, thinking that it ought to be decided mainly by the consideration, what great improvement in the life and culture stands next in order for the people concerned, as the condition of their further progress, and what institutions are most likely to promote that...
I thought the predominance of the aristocratic classes, the noble and the rich...an evil worth any struggle to get rid of...because it made the conduct of the government an example of gross public immorality, through the predominance of private over public interests in the state, and the abuse of the powers of legislation for the advantage of classes...while the higher and richer classes held the power of government, the instruction and improvement of the mass of the people were contrary to the self-interest of those classes, because tending to render the people more powerful for throwing off the yoke." (J.S. Mill; *Autobiography*, 1873).

"This disposition to admire...the rich and powerful, and...to neglect persons of poor and mean condition, *though necessary both to establish and to maintain the distinction of ranks and the order of society,* **is...the great and most universal cause of the corruption of our moral**

sentiments." (Adam Smith; *Theory of Moral Sentiments, 1759*, Chap. 3) (Emphasis added).

Italicized is the admission that the *admiration and acceptance* of the rich and powerful is the great cause of moral corruption in human society; that moral sentiments erode when the equality of rights is forsaken by those most in need of them:

"...and the wondering cheated multitude worshipped the invention." (Thomas Paine; Rights of Man, March 16, 1791).

Convince a man that the appearance of superiority to which he defers is not by nature, or some divine will, but only by human invention, established on no legitimacy other than the fact of possession, and whose origin was no more than by presumption and appropriation by force, and he may reconsider his deference.

. . . .

Few things are more self-evident than the natural entitlement of Nature's creatures to the materials that Nature has provided for their survival and development; *no right exists for any person or social system to decide that some get more and some get less.* Yet human culture has forever been dominated by the fearful brain's greed for more than its share... its desire to deprive others to secure and enrich itself. The Declaration asserts that government is to *secure* the unalienable rights of life for all, not to facilitate a winner-take-most competition that rewards and reinforces the selfish brain... a competition that drives the individual into psychological alienation from a common humanity. (Indeed, competition for security is an oxymoron).

Private property is justified as a natural right to the exclusive possession of the material conditions that sustain the individual life, *not as an unlimited accumulation of those materials that denies the natural entitlement of others*. That private property is a natural right serving a common interest in preserving an independent life and in preventing social conflict over resources, also means that the regulation and limitation of property is necessary to prevent the establishment of social inequalities that also inevitably foment resentments and conflict. Equality of rights and social harmony, and the appeal of moral sentiments among those who have them, both justify *and limit* private property. The natural law limit on the extent of private ownership is: that none have a right to more unless all have a right to enough.

"Men, being once born, have a right to their Preservation, and consequently to Meat and Drink, and such other things, as Nature affords for their Subsistence." (John Locke; *Two Treatises of Government,* 1689, Book 2, Ch 5).

"...no Man could ever have a just Power over the life of another by Right of property in Land or Possessions." (ibid. Book1, Ch 4).

"Self-love will make Men partial to themselves and their Friends... Government to restrain the partiality and violence of Men...*Civil Government* is the proper Remedy

for the Inconveniences of the Sate of Nature." (ibid. Book 2, Ch 2).

Property rights fixed in law in a manner that allows the separation of citizens into classes of unequal privilege and unequal power is an approval of social inequality by civil law; and is a direct contravention of the **"created equal"** principle, circumventing the declared equalities of natural law and liberal democracy through the achieved inequalities of liberal economics: *Classical and neoliberal economics undermines liberal democracy* by giving freedom to anti-democratic ambitions, allowing achieved wealth to control government for its own interest, not the common good. And therein lies the core contradiction within liberalism: the two primary principles of "liberalism" are *equality* and *freedom* (also called liberty, continuing the confusion). Thus, in practice, liberal political and social equality are sabotaged by neoliberal economic "freedom." Which leads to the political divide: the humanitarian brain assigns priority to human equality (progressives, left liberals); the selfish, resistance-to-equality brain upholds the freedom to achieve inequality (neoliberals, conservatives, libertarians, and centrist liberals). For the conservative brain, the advantaged side of inequality is sanctuary from its amygdala fears. If human equality is to be realized there can be no freedom to deny it.

Successful economic activity does not require a class divided society. There is a distinction between the economics of production and the private wealth that is extracted from it... and the former does not necessitate the latter—extreme profits could as easily reward the investment of labor as the investment of money... money deserving no more than the payment of interest. A conscientious desire to create and build and self-express and enhance one's well-being while contributing to the common good, is as capable of producing economic growth as the "animal spirits" of unregulated greed and selfish ambitions. The incentives offered by neoliberal ideology, in the absence of moral conscience, are a *free*way to political and financial *corruption. Freedom is judged by the passions it sets free... and the consequences they covet... the freer the greed of id, the less possible the dreams of superego.

*(See the Panama and Paradise and Pandora Papers, and FinCen Files, and all the shell corporations and tax laws and financial havens that facilitate evasion... providing equal opportunity for corruption).

"...commercial interest tends to 'suffocate' spiritual life in principle, moral imperatives are not adhered to in politics... The notion of freedom has been diverted to unbridled passion, in other words, in the direction of the forces of evil (so that nobody's "freedom" would be limited!). (Alexander Solzhenitsyn; Harvard, 8 June 1978) (Parenthesis in original).

To be clear, it is not the economic freedom of the individual to secure his livelihood by his own talent and effort through business enterprise, nor is it the efficiency and allocation principles of the free market that necessarily subvert democracy, *but the logically inescapable end-achievements of unequal wealth, power, and privilege that result from a failure to regulate self-interested economic behavior for democratic outcomes*. Deregulation and tax cuts and small government (**"Government is the**

problem") are the cries of the fear-based brain, greedily wishing to escape the implications of **"created equal."**

("Fear-based brain" does not refer to the *feeling* of fear. The emotion of fear in discussing brain function refers to the *unconscious* reflex of the amygdala to sensory information from the environment perceived as threat; whereupon the amygdala sends alarms to other brain regions which initiate various physiological and neurological responses. When all this is occurring in the very early years of life brain structure and function are profoundly affected—neurons are building the circuits and memories that will form our personality and prejudices, deciding who we become. And when the fear emotion is excessive the structure of conservative anti-other, xenophobic selfishness is being formed. The *feeling* of fear occurs when the neocortex consciously receives the alarm message and agrees there is reason to be afraid—or has the neural strength and moral faculty to disagree. It is not claimed here that the pursuers of wealth hoarding and anti-democratic dominance feel afraid... they are well conditioned to feel secure in their entitlements... until a democratic people awaken to democracy's promise.)

....

A society that professes the principle of equality, yet embraces a systemic pathway to inequality is guilty of moral and political apostasy. Progressive taxation of inordinate wealth and income is consistent with "free-market" arrangements, and can easily remedy the inequality that the **"invisible hand"** and **"spontaneous order"** were, and are, too willing to allow—and too determined to maintain. The argument over capitalism and socialism is worse than useless; it is a name-calling distraction from critical thought. The resolution of social injustice lies in the balance between private enterprise rewards and the social investments that would realize the natural entitlements of all individuals; a balance that would also provide a favorable base for a rightfully regulated market—an educated, psychologically and materially secured population, a protected environment, research and development. Private enterprise and its market efficiencies, and opportunities for independence and self-expression, are rightfully made free, and rightfully restricted to outcomes consistent with democratic principles and the common good. The profit above costs of production—fair salaries, wages, plant and material inputs, and interest on capital—would more rightfully return to the benefit of community than to the creation of private wealth. *Free market principles do not require greatly unequal outcomes.* If cupidity feels disincentivized so much the better, for that is the point.

It is not good, nor is it freedom, that the government should own the private economy; nor is it good or freedom that the private economy should own the government. *In a democracy the rights of the sovereign people overrule both.*

The business interest lies in maximizing profit; which involves minimizing the compensation to labor, and maximizing the price consumption will bear. The interests are not common: the laborer would like a higher wage, and the consumer would like a lower price. Both would increase the general well-being. But the business owner wants to increase his wealth—*price setting and cost cutting will always adjust to maintain or expand inequality. Competition is not a trustworthy savior against the consolidation of economic power.* It falls to wise and just regulation to balance the natural rights and freedoms of individuals—cognitive intelligence in service to human rights instead of sociopathic wants.

The dynamic of private economic enterprise is thus based on a conflict of interests: the desire for increased general well-being, the common interest, versus the pursuit of private wealth, the individual interest. A democratic government's purpose is to guard the common welfare by preventing an accumulation of private wealth and power that violates democratic principles. The democratic resolution: private enterprise is good, but it cannot have bad consequences upon human equality and the common good. Most egregiously, vast wealth draws limited resources away from more essential social goods into the production of objects of vanity for the gratification of avarice.

Neoliberalism claimed there would be no bad consequences, that the profits of private enterprise flowing to the upper class would "trickle down" to the lower classes, minimizing wealth inequality... let the rich get richer and maybe the poor will get less poor. But the neoliberal plan was to weaken collective bargaining and dismantle government regulation, so there would be no countervailing forces to assure a fair distribution of wealth; trickle down would be at the discretion of those accumulating the wealth. What followed were decades of tax cuts, deregulation and wealth consolidation (the accelerated Republican agenda since Reagan). Tax cutting, in particular, was the mechanism for the accumulation of wealth; along with the U.S. Supreme Court giving corporations personhood, providing free speech protection to the political use of money in *purchasing* policy and politicians… and the monopolization of media to propagandize public opinion. Neoliberalism is not the friend of democracy and the Rights of Man.

The selfish brain treats veracity—truth, honesty and principle—as an option; and expediency as a first principle. The barrier to a truly *created equal* democracy lies in a failure to understand and confront the true intentions of the selfish brain:

"[The] children of light recognized the existence of a moral law beyond themselves...But all were naive about the power of self-interest in society...naivete made the children of light inept at defending democracy against the children of darkness...The children of darkness, being cunning and immoral in their pursuit of power, better understood the centrality of will-to-power in politics and history." (Reinhold Niebuhr; *The Children of Light and The Children of Darkness*, 1944).

The defeat of evil will ultimately require a democratic choice between the children compelled to darkness (id) and the children open to the light (superego).

Edmond Burke:

"Men qualify for civil liberty (freedom) **in exact proportion to their disposition *to put moral chains upon their own appetites*; in proportion as their love of justice is above their rapacity... Society cannot exist unless a controlling power upon the will and appetite be placed somewhere, and *the less of it there is within, the more there must be without*...men of intemperate minds cannot be free. Their passions forge their fetters."** (*Letter to a*

Member of the French Assembly; January 19, 1791)
(Emphasis and parenthesis added).

"The modern trouble is in a low capacity to believe in *precepts which restrict and restrain private interests and desire.* **Conviction of the need of these restraints is difficult to restore...We must renew the convictions from which our political morality springs."** (Walter Lippmann; *The Public Philosophy*, Book 2, ch. 9) (Emphasis added).

"The best lack all conviction, while the worst are full of passionate intensity." (Yeats; *The Second Coming*, 1921).

. . . .

Individuals gather into groups and societies for a security of their lives not achievable individually. And by doing so, each must consent to the renunciation of their individual actions (*freedom*) that would infringe upon the equal rights and security of others. The essence of the democratic covenant is community respect for the rights of the individual, and the individual's reciprocal obligation to the good of the community:

"...by these presents, [we do] solemnly and mutually... covenant and combine ourselves together into a civil politic; *for our better ordering, and preservation...* **and by virtue hereof to enact, constitute, and frame, such** *just and equal laws,* **ordinances, acts, constitutions, and offices...as shall be thought most meet and convenient for** *the general good of the colony; unto which we promise all due submission and obedience."* (*Mayflower Compact*; November 11, 1620) (Emphasis added).

"But every man, when he enters into society, gives up a part of his natural liberty, as the price of so valuable a purchase; and, in consideration of receiving the advantages of mutual commerce, obliges himself *to conform to those laws, which the community has thought proper to establish*. And this species of legal obedience and conformity is infinitely more desirable than that wild and savage liberty which is sacrificed to obtain it. For no man that considers a moment would wish to retain the absolute and uncontrolled power of doing whatever he pleases: the consequence of which is, that every other man would also have the same power, and then there *would be no security* to individuals in any of the enjoyments of life. Political, therefore, or civil liberty, which is that of a member of society, is no other than natural liberty *so far restrained by human laws* (and no farther) as is necessary and expedient *for the general advantage of the public*. Hence we may collect that the law, which restrains a man from doing mischief to his fellow-citizens, though it diminishes the natural, **increases the civil liberty of mankind."** (Blackstone; *Commentaries*; Book 1, Chap 1) (Parenthesis in original; Emphasis added).

"We the People of the United States, in Order to form a more perfect Union, establish Justice, insure domestic Tranquility, provide for the common defense, promote the general welfare, and secure the blessings of liberty to ourselves and our posterity, do ordain and establish this Constitution for the United States of America." (Preamble to the Constitution of the United States of America).

The phrases of the Preamble—We the People, perfect Union, establish Justice, domestic Tranquility, common defense, general welfare, secure the blessings of liberty—speak *to the common goods of all*, not the freedoms of individuals.

The central imperative of a social covenant is to establish a binding union of one people under one nation, to which all give allegiance for their common security and benefit. Patriotism to one's country means loyalty and deference to its founding covenant—for the gift of both freedom and liberty gained.

There are two indispensable principles to democracy's promise: one, that sovereignty lies at the bottom, a possession of all the people; and two, that individual freedom is subordinate to the social contract, the covenantal agreement for mutual protection and benefit. Unregulated capitalist economics violates mutual protection and benefit by fostering social inequality; and also, through the influence of financial wealth, transfers political power to the beneficiaries of that inequality; allowing the irony of democracy's procedures being used to erode democracy's promise—a plutocratic overthrow of democracy from within.

Politics, then, is a battle between the superego's pursuit of a "more perfect union," and id's scheming for advantage and control of governmental policy. Progressivism wishes to legislate policies that achieve the promised end; conservatism wishes to preserve or impose policies that deliver the end it wants—social and financial inequality.

I will not harm you if you will not harm me is the foundational pledge of human society; it is the basis of morality and trust and obligation, and of mutual expectations of fairness, with the primary purpose of eliminating violent conflict and resource insecurity. Although the individual is not obliged to do good to others—that is for the quality of his conscience to decide—he is strictly called not to do harm; not to engage means or achieve ends that obstruct the full and just implications of **"created equal."** Democratic government is not for the purpose of securing freedom for individual transgressions against common security and equality. *Government is to secure rights—protect liberty—not enable or accept transgressions as a consequence of freedom.* The equal right to life, and the equal liberty of the rights and entitlements of life, require a prohibition against any substantial inequality in the *conditions* of life.

The security of life and the rights of life require the rule of laws. Whether it be a law against murder or a law requiring one to drive on the right-hand side of the road, all laws are restrictions on individual freedom for the common good. The selfish ambition for privileged position is a betrayal of social trust—a failure to respect the equal worth of others. The bonds of consensual society are not fashioned for the achievement and protection of privilege, but upon a promise of mutual security, by sharing the fruit of the tree.

Societies would not exist if social traits did not enhance the survival of the individual; the individual has adapted to social organization because he has better survived through cooperation and sympathy with others, a truth thus affirmed by *natural selection*—but unacknowledged by the selfish brain. The individualist and libertarian uphold the selfish trait, minimizing mutual obligation and social interdependence, resenting regulation of the individual's freedom. But respect for the freedom and moral worth of the individual does not require a disregard for the good of others and the community as a whole; nor does it justify opposition to a government that pursues the good of all citizens. *It is selfishness absent humanitarian values and sentiments that disdains compassion and regard for the equality of others.* Indeed, it is the very moral worth of each individual, as expressed in **"created equal,"** that demands equality for all... that no person be consigned to social inferiority as a result of the desires and decisions of others. Freedom of individual choice is not the issue around which Individualism is criticized: it is the attitude that commonly lies behind the demand for unregulated freedom—dismissal of mutual obligation, and indifference to unjust circumstances and harmful consequences. What diminishes the moral quality of the individual is his disregard for others. Society does not begin as an agreement to protect the freedom of the selfish individual, but to restrain it:

Alexis de Tocqueville made these truly insightful observations about selfishness and individualism:

"Selfishness originates in blind instinct (the amygdala's fear); **individualism proceeds from erroneous judgment** (frontal cortex complicit with the amygdala) **more than from depraved feelings; it originates as much in deficiencies of mind** (undeveloped empathic faculty) **as in perversity of heart... Selfishness blights the germ of all virtue: individualism, at first, only saps the virtues of**

public life (bitter partisanship)**; but, in the long run, it attacks and destroys all others, and is at length absorbed in downright selfishness."** (*Democracy in America*, 1835; book 2, chapter 2) (Parentheses added).

"Despotism, which is of a very timorous nature (an overly fearful amygdala), **is never more secure of continuance than when it can keep men asunder** (by imposing economic and political inequality); **and all its influence is commonly exerted for that purpose** (compulsive advantage seeking, unremitting greed). **No vice of the human heart is so acceptable to it as selfishness..."** (ibid. book 2, chapter 3) (Parentheses added).

"It must therefore be expected that personal interest will become more than ever the principal if not the sole spring of men's actions; but it remains to be seen how each man will understand his personal interest...no one can foretell into what disgrace and wretchedness they would plunge themselves lest they should have to sacrifice something of their own well-being to the prosperity of their fellow creatures." (ibid. chapter 8).

Jefferson also:

"To me then it appears that there have been differences of opinion, and party differences, from the first establishment of governments, to the present day...that everyone takes his side in favor of the many (humanitarian), **or the few** (selfish), *according to his constitution, and the circumstances in which he is placed* (genetic level of fear and environmental conditioning) **...the terms of whig [sic] and tory [sic] belong to natural, as**

well as civil history. They denote the temper and *constitution of mind* (brain function and structure) **of different individuals."** (Thomas Jefferson; *Letter to John Adams*, June 27, 1813) (Emphasis and parenthesis added).

John Stuart Mill:

"Interest in the common good is at present so weak a motive in the generality, not because it can never be otherwise, but because the mind is not accustomed to dwell on it as it dwells from morning till night on things which tend only to personal advantage...The deep-rooted selfishness which forms the general character of the existing state of society, is so deeply rooted, only because the whole course of existing institutions tends to foster it." (Cultural conditioning). (*Autobiography*, 1873) (Emphasis and parenthesis added).

"...we see that avarice, anger, pride and stupidity commonly profit far beyond charity, modesty, justice and thought." (Thomas More; 1478-1535).

"...the egoistic corruption of universal ideals is a much more persistent fact in human conduct than any moralistic creed is inclined to admit." (Reinhold Niebuhr; *The Children of Light and The Children of Darkness*, 1944, Ch 1).

Neoliberalism is not endorsed by the principles expressed in The Declaration of Independence; neoliberal democracy is not The Declaration's democracy.

. . . .

Selfishness is not a new thing: it is the original, primal thing; an instinctual reaction to threat, or opportunity for gain or pleasure. In the selfish brain it remains an emotion--an emotion supported, rather than moderated, by a complicit prefrontal cortex devising cognitive strategies to *combat its fears and achieve its desires*. Even if social affinity was not a factor in man's nature, reason would quickly realize that killing each other is not a sustainable exercise of self-interest. A rational self-interest would favor less *a freedom to kill* and more *a liberty from being killed—*survival seems better achieved by agreeing not to kill each other than hurrying to kill first. The nature of man can be whatever the environment allows it to be. The environment, natural or social, does not require competitive conflict. It is man's amygdala master and his moral dysfunction that propels him into selfish competitions for advantage. A conservative think tank is a collection of alarmed amygdalae conspiring to obstruct the advancement of liberty and justice for all.

In past times the right to rule was presumed to rest on divine prescription, or right of conquest. Classical liberalism introduced the regime of competition... material wealth, political power, and ruling class membership would be achieved—and "merited"—by victory in free competition; to which everyone, it was asserted, had an "equal opportunity." Competition is a euphemism for conflict, implying outcomes are fair and not coercive or arbitrary. *If democratic equality is a first principle, then extreme inequality, however achieved, is not justifiable, and thus cannot be merited.* Unlimited private property and economic competition permit the denial of natural entitlement; competition for economic wellness means many will be confined to less than wellness... the punishment for "losing" being hardship for families and impaired mental development for children.

When competition is the only means of gaining livelihood everyone will be required to play the game... adaptation for survival. The game makes the players play; and when it is the only game (**"There-Is-No-Alternative"**), and it denies natural entitlement, *it is coercive and arbitrary*.

Democracy's principle of equality precludes all rationalizations of social inequality—the attempts of the selfish brain to justify economic and political hegemony. Accumulation of property and power through competition is no more democratically acceptable as a path to social dominance, than conquest or birthright or divine decree. Class superiority is aristocracy, not democracy. It is class division itself that is evil... upon whatever pretext it is established.

The only legitimate power to rule is democratic—a limited and temporary and revocable delegation, not a possession by any prior right... **"Governments are instituted among Men, deriving their just powers from the consent of the governed."** Official office holders of whatever level are employees of the sovereign people.

The selfish brain is eager for benefits, less eager for obligation; it finds self-preservation by exploiting the advantages of community while minimizing its own contribution. Individualism proclaims self-reliance and non-dependence, but it has never been the power to stand alone in the wild. Few if any creatures are more naturally insufficient than Homo sapiens; nor more dependent on the contributions of their kind. Humans have survived and prospered by shared invention and recognition of a common interest in the security of their lives. The selfish brain rejects mutual obligation... it believes it ought to do what it wants for itself, discounting the enormous structure of support provided by the community. The ethical brain wants to do what it ought, obedient to principles and values that transcend personal interest (which includes many principled conservatives). It is the divide that turns politics over policies for achieving common goals and mutual well-being into the politics of partisan advantage... in denial and opposition to common goals. The progressive's commitment to equality and social justice is not a denial of individuality, it is a demand for the equality of all individuals—even the selfish ones.

Selfishness is the primal instinct; cooperation is the evolved understanding that socioeconomic competition for well-being is a pre-violence conflict, until unjust outcomes call forth violent redress. The effort required to remedy wrongs is justified by the effort exerted in the defense of wrongs. That injustice be rectified is the prevailing imperative.

"...evil is always the assertion of some self-interest without regard to the whole...the good is...always the harmony of the whole." (Reinhold Niebuhr; *The Children of Light and The Children of Darkness,* 1944).

It can fairly be said there are two precepts, or assertions, of Individualism: that the individual has a natural right to pursue his desires; and also, a right not to be subordinated to the demands of others. These precepts express an inconsistency, and also exemplify the distinction between freedom and liberty. The right not to be subordinated to the demands of others imposes a restriction on the freedom of others to pursue desires that would subordinate another. The inconsistency is: you cannot have both equally—you cannot have a right to do whatever *you want*, and also a right of protection from what *others want*... which reveals the inherent hypocrisy of the selfish brain; and also displays the distinction: "liberty" is the right not to be unjustly subordinated that limits the "freedom" that would subordinate. The neoliberal subordination of *liberty* in favor of the predominance of *freedom*—by the synonymous use of the terms—is how social inequality is orchestrated, and ostensibly justified.

Libertarian Individualism is likely a behavioral selfishness resulting from emotional/psychological separation due to the amygdala's genetic fear of others—a lack of empathetic connection to others and community; or perhaps an absence of emotional warmth in early childhood; a psychological isolation seeking rationalization as a freedom philosophy.

Injustice is the social denial of the rights that derive from natural entitlement; which are construed in relation to the stage of cultural and technological development of a given society. The social entitlements ("safety nets") of neoliberal society are but minimal attempts at recompense for the systemic cultivation of social inequality—the denial of natural entitlement—by providing a nickel where a dollar is due; lessening starvation in the streets without restricting the opportunity for extravagance.

The unequal possession of wealth and power originates in history by arbitrary and coercive appropriation, not by any right to superior status or possession. No person ever conceded knowingly to, or preferred, a deprived and inferior status... an unequal right to a good life. Nor does silent submission imply tacit consent. Only the machinations of mercenary philosophers aiming to justify a preferred circumstance could ever conceive a tacit common consent to social inferiority. And although a long history of enforcement has made inequality a tradition for some and a confinement for others, *it has never made it a right—and what is unjustly done is never unjustly undone.*

Also, it is not enough that the privileged man appears sympathetic, or even generous to the unprivileged, if he also defends his right to be privileged. The issue is privilege itself, the presumption of a right to be superior and advantaged, and to maintain the unprivileged in a place of subordination. The most insidious dissemble is the public expression of sympathy that privately—and politically—opposes a remedy of the wrong.

It is commonplace for the defenders of privilege and advantage to oppose remedies by calling them unjust, as if removing privileges and advantages is a more grievous act than imposing them. To declare it unjust to lessen inequality (as in taxing wealth) is to assert the justice of inequality; it is turning justice on its head... the authors of injustice defining themselves as victims. *Justice is not found in the opinions of transgressors*; and injustice is not made right because it has long existed.

And so, freedom of the individual is not the first purpose of civil society, but the security of the common rights of all people. Thus, natural rights do not imply limited government, they imply government sufficient to secure natural rights. Natural rights do not free individual selfishness from regulation, they protect individuals from subjection to undemocratic powers, public and private—*liberty is protection from power, not a right to possess power.* The purview of government is, therefore, determined by the prevalence and persistence of the injustice it must oppose—as in the assault by economic inequality upon democratic equality.

"Government is instituted for the common good; for the protection, safety, prosperity, and happiness of the people; and not for profit, honor, or private interest of any one man, family, or class of men..." (John Adams; *Thoughts on Government*, 1776).

....

The first concern of life is survival, so behavior toward self-preservation is a natural right. The social covenant requires that self-preservation not be achieved through behaviors that harm others. Thus, the democratic purpose of a national economy is to employ the efforts of all its citizens and to distribute a fair and equitable well-being to all, and not to allow the formation of class divisions between its people.

It is argued here that classical liberal (and neoliberal) economic ideology denies government's role in securing the rights that follow from natural entitlement, making the materials and conditions of life's sustenance not a right, but an "opportunity," achievable through "success" in a competitive struggle in which only a minority will "succeed;" with government securing not the rights of all, but the results of the struggle for the few; subordinating the rights of life to the right to wealth and dominance... *The natural rights of life are not the rewards of victory in competition.* The outcomes of economic competition must be regulated so that winning is not luxury and domination, and losing is not deprivation and subordination.

The call for less government is a call for less justice, less protection of natural rights, *less restraint upon the ambitions of the selfish brain.* It is a call for **"...government of the people, by the people, for the people..."** to be too weak to achieve its purpose. The freedom of the individual is a high moral imperative, but it is not the highest. The highest law is the protection (liberty) of the innocent life; that the natural entitlements of life are assured, and the security of life well-guarded.

The natural right of a child to realize her life's potential must never be limited by the depriving conditions of her birth environment; whether that deprivation is imposed by societal systems or parental inadequacy. A child's life belongs to the child, not to the parents of the child. Parental rights, therefore, are subordinate to the child's inalienable right to a life of self-realization; implying the right not to be developmentally limited by parental or cultural indoctrination. The parental role is more a matter of responsibility and obligation to the child than rights over her.

The political principles of "created equal" and "right to life" have priority over the arrangements and consequences of economic freedom—socioeconomic institutions must pursue, not obstruct, the political end. It is moral nonsense to suppose the freedom of one to gain wealth justifies the economic hardship of many. The three great obstacles to overcoming human inequality are the freedom to achieve it, the power to enforce it, and the acquiescence that endures it.

"Wherever there is great property there is great inequality. For one very rich man there must be at least five hundred poor, and the affluence of the few supposes the indigence of the many...It is only under the shelter of the civil magistrate that the owner of that valuable property...can sleep a single night in security...The acquisition of valuable and extensive property, therefore, necessarily requires the establishment of civil government... The rich, in particular, are necessarily interested to support that order of things which can alone secure them in the possession of their own advantages...civil government, so far as it is instituted for the security of property, is in reality instituted for the defense of the rich against the poor, or of those who have some property against those who have none at all." (Adam Smith; *The Wealth of Nations*; bk. 5, ch.1).

"It is not...difficult to foresee which of the two parties must... have the advantage...and force the other into a compliance with their terms." (ibid. bk.1, ch.8).

"The proposal of any new law or regulation of commerce which comes from this order (the business interest) ought always to be listened to with great precaution... It comes from an *order of men* (the selfish brain) whose interest is never exactly the same with that of the public, who have generally an interest to deceive and even to oppress the public, and who accordingly, have upon many occasions, both deceived and oppressed it." (ibid. bk.1, ch.11) (Parenthesis and emphasis added).

"…those different plans were, perhaps, first introduced by the private interests and prejudices of particular orders of men, without any regard to, or foresight of, their consequences upon the general welfare of the society…" (ibid.).

"Wealth, as Mr. Hobbes says, is power." (ibid. bk.1, ch.5)

The prophet of a free enterprise economy openly stated that wealth requires poverty; and perfectly described the control of government by the money interest... *thus the antithetical relationship between capitalism's purpose and democracy's promise.* Unregulated capitalism creates a pyramid of wealth, wide hardship at the bottom, a narrow pinnacle of opulence at the top. *So where is the principle and reasoning that justifies the privileged affluence of the few and the struggling subsistence of the many?*

In *The Wealth of Nations*, Adam Smith argued for releasing the productive power of natural self-interest for achieving economic growth. But hidden behind the *evolved* instinct for self-preservation of the unselfish mind was the *unevolved* reptilian brain, whose lack of ethical conscience no **"invisible hand"** would restrain. Beside the virtuous man who calls for freedom stands the rapacious man who sees freedom as an *opportunity* for unjust exploitations. Rapacity's advantage is found in virtue's tolerance, or naive underestimation:

"…the social idealism which informs our democratic civilization had a touching faith in the possibility of achieving a simple harmony between self-interest and the general welfare…they proved to be mistaken. They did

not make the mistake, however, of giving simple moral sanction to self-interest. They depended rather upon *controls and restraints which proved to be inadequate.*" (Reinhold Niebuhr; ibid. ch 1) (Emphasis added—a reference to what has come to be the inadequate regulation of classical liberalism.)

"...is the disposition to imposture so prevalent in men of experience, that their private views of ambition and avarice can be accomplished only by artifice?... There is nothing in which mankind have been more unanimous; yet nothing can be inferred from it more than this, that the multitude have always been credulous, and the few artful." (John Adams; *A Defense of the Constitutions...* 1787, Preface).

Neoliberalism supposes government's purpose to be the defense of a freedom to achieve inequality; The Declaration of Independence declares government to be the guardian of equal rights. Hence, the failed promise: the moral ethos of democratic equality betrayed by the selfish ethos of aristocratic inequality; the inherent schizophrenia of capitalist democracy—the neurological and political dichotomies between the humanitarian brain and the fear-inspired selfish brain. The issue is in the adjective: Are we a *capitalistic* democracy or a *democratic* capitalism?

. . . .

Natural law is the biological force—**"the Laws of Nature and of Nature's God"**—that gives life to all creatures, and provides the means of their sustenance. Natural entitlement is the inherent natural and unalienable right to nature's provisions. Natural community is the social arrangement of laws and institutions that fulfill each person's natural rights. **"Created equal"** is the indispensable recognition of mutual birthright that makes social inequality a transgression against creation.

The Declaration's phrase **"created equal"** does not assert that persons are born equal in all their characteristics and capacities: some will be taller, smarter, prettier, and run faster. Biological creation is not equal. Equal creation is a declaration by covenant that all persons are to be vested with moral and social equality as a first principle ("**We hold these truths to be self-evident**"); that they are equal in personhood by virtue of natural creation, regardless of biological variation (no less would be consensual). *The declaration of **"created equal"** as a self-evident truth entails a promise of remaining commensurate in society.* There is no point in proclaiming equal creation unless it is a moral and political commitment to remain substantially equal in fact. If not, it was a frivolous declaration, or literary exuberance to fit the occasion... or would you believe the declaration of equality to be a mere dissemblance by the Founding Fathers intending to enlist popular support for the independence only of the colonial elite? Politicians are known for their insincere assurances. But given the gravity of the time, and the enormity of the task, it is stretching cynicism to ascribe insincerity to the dedication of their **"lives, fortunes, and sacred honor."** Of course, that all *men* were created equal was a more literal and tolerable declaration to 1776 social reality; but the Founders were too intelligent not to be aware they were committing to *principles with transcendent implications.*

Whatever erodes democracy is **"destructive of these ends."** Further, even where a degree of privileged condition is granted by public acceptance in recognition of an individual's contribution to the common good, personal merit is not transferable to associates or heirs, neither then would be the privileges and possessions it gained. **"Created equal"** implies a limitation on inequality, and *certainly a prohibition against bequeathing it*. When practice creates conditions that deviate from a founding principle, it is a wrong practice.

On reflection, what behaviors are meritorious? Is compulsive greed deserving of great reward? Are rapacious ambitions? And remorseless selfishness? Are the achievements of corruption and deceit worthy of being retained? All these unethical traits of character are set free and rewarded by the neoliberal maxim of unregulated freedom. *And the **"spontaneous order"** they create is not democracy's promise.*

It is axiomatic that selfishness will favor itself when given a choice. That choice, when it furthers inequality, is an anti-democratic freedom. A system that elevates selfishness to positions of authority has no **"invisible hand"** favoring justice. The good of a community must be achieved by the intentions of goodwill, not by unintended happenstances.

Aggressive ambitions driven by excessive emotional reactions to primordial fears, or insatiable desires to possess the objects of pleasure, are not the expressions of a superior brain, but a disordered brain; a brain with a regrettable genetic plan, or harmfully conditioned by early environmental impositions. It is a brain that does not deserve greater reward and satisfaction than a brain of more moderate ambitions. *"Animal spirits" are not an excuse for escaping the requirements of justice; they are the reason for just requirements.*

No human physiological or neurological characteristic "merits" unequal power and privilege, no more than the tallest man deserves more fruit from the tree because he has the longest reach. Inequality is a presumption by those who think themselves superior, historically imposed by force or by the guile of malevolent persuasions. The problem with human character is not insufficient self-esteem, it is the inflated esteem of the narcissist who thinks himself deserving of superiority.

A society that further benefits those born to natural or family advantages with social superiority, and further punishes those less advantaged with sustained inferiority, is a mean society. Those with advantages proclaim "equal opportunity" to justify their advantage. When advantage is unequal opportunity is unequal. "Opportunity" implicitly concedes that all will not succeed; and disadvantage assures it.

"...the phrase equality of opportunity...is the impertinent courtesy of an invitation offered to unwelcome guests, in the certainty that circumstances will prevent them from accepting it." (R.H. Tawney; *Equality,* 1931, chap. 3).

Perhaps the greatest human illusion is the conceit of selfish ego—pride in the achievement of advantage, *as if the need of advantage is a strength.* A modest opinion of oneself, along with gratitude and generosity are the virtues of a mind that has gained true self-awareness of its ultimate dependence on Nature's provisions and a cooperative community. What we think we have individually achieved is largely the work of capacities given to us by *genetic generosity* and the experiences of care and guidance provided to us by a supportive and educating early-life environment, applied to the accumulated accomplishments of countless generations before us.

Personality and intelligence emerge from a blend of genetic and environmental determinants, and when fortunate they are *gifts, not personal achievements*. It is the nature of happenstance that coincidental and chance occurrences of time and place, invitations and open doors—or rejections and closed doors—and who one knows or happens to meet, conspire to greatly benefit some and greatly deprive others. The obtrusive personality of a sociopath, in the game of social politics, is often advanced and rewarded over quiet and unpretentious good-will and competence.

Genetic and environmental circumstances produce capability; greater equality in circumstances would produce greater equality in capability. We are each the product of a developmental process composed of events and circumstances we did not choose. People do not choose to be autistic or depressive; neither do they choose to be exceptionally talented; some people are born with genetic handicaps; many are born into destructive environments; some are born into both. And some are born with great advantages that they think are achievements. *No one is self-made... fate decides.*

"There but for the grace of God go I." (The humility proverb).

Especially egregious are the efforts of the advantaged to arrange systemic circumstances that favor the chosen and obstruct the progress and participation of others... the very nature of class society... the very intention of neoliberal elites. To conceive and conspire for such a purpose, and not have the moral sensibility to care about the lives of others, is the heart of evil. Neoliberalism—unregulated free-market economy—both rewards and punishes much more than is ever deserved.

As advantages are rarely equal, neither are the good fortunes of happenstance. The destiny of each of us is subject to **"the power of fortune"** (David Hume).

....

Natural evolution is a biological process whereby the physical and behavioral characteristics of living organisms change over time through a process of genetic mutation. *Mutation* is a random event that alters the structure and expression of genes, creating a *variation* in physical and behavioral traits; it is biological happenstance.

Natural selection is the mechanism by which the mutations--genetic variations--that enhance the organism's survival within a given environment are transferred to succeeding generations through reproduction. The process whereby the organism is successfully adjusting to the environment, either through physical or behavioral changes, is called *adaptation*; the environment is, in effect, dictating the structure and function and content of the developing brain. The brain is thus a product of its surroundings, both natural and social. (The implications for notions of freewill and self-determination are endless).

Survival security, then, depends on achieving and maintaining a beneficial harmony with the immediate environment. And the more dependent the individual brain is on a particular environment, due to its level of primal fear and the degree of physical security and emotional reassurance gained from that environment, the more sensitive and resistant it will be to changes in that environment; not only in defense of physical survival, but also in defense of political and social advantages.

Environmental determinism is why social ranks and cultural separation are so persistent—different environments make different people. Even before birth the brain is forming prospective synaptic connections, potential developmental pathways to full self-realization. Our early environmental experiences will select which neural circuits are strengthened to determine who we become, and which are eliminated to rob us of who we might have been. The angel or the reptile, which doorway is opened and which closed is not our choice.

So, what if the organism must adapt to a changing environment without the aid of a beneficial mutation? What if the organism must "choose" to change, adapt through advisability rather than by passive natural selection? Does an organism highly dependent on an existing environment for survival security have the neural flexibility, and moral discernment, to adapt to the challenge of a changing environment? This question is at the base of society's politics—a brain open to accepting change toward greater justice and common security versus opposition to change because of the brain's emotional dependency on existing conditions, however unjust; even resisting highly advisable changes in the face of global warming.

"A conservative is someone who stands athwart history, yelling 'stop!'" (William F. Buckley, Jr.).

Natural selection is not a value judgment, it does not say which physical and behavioral traits ought to survive, only which traits have survived an existing environment; physical survival does not imply moral or qualitative superiority of the organism:

"The law is not the survival of the 'better' or the 'stronger'...It is the survival of those which are constitutionally fittest to thrive under the conditions in which they are placed; and very often that which, *humanly speaking, is inferiority*, causes the survival." (Herbert Spencer; *Principles of Biology*, 1864) (Emphasis added).

*Neoliberal culture selects selfishness, greed, and expediency over a sensibility for equality and morality—that is, traits that are **"humanly speaking,"** inferior.*

Natural selection is not random. It is environment dependent, subject to environmental conditions. A different environment would support the selection of different traits. Fish have a survival advantage in water, not so much on mountain tops (above water mountain tops!). Selfish ambitions are advantaged in competitive and morally lax environments, but not so much among friends; that is, friends who are not hopelessly deferential, thus encouraging the egocentric personality (A common moral weakness of the human brain is the deferential, even reverential creation of celebrities; conceding the center of attention to those who presume it).

It is a major purpose of this hypothesis to emphasize that *social* evolution offers an opportunity for improvement, progress to a more life enhancing experience for all people; purposeful changes in the social environment that select and reinforce more humanitarian brain sensibilities—assuming the mental flexibility to overcome prior cultural conditioning, and to escape the amygdala fear that generates hate toward different others, and to find the courage to choose morality. Indeed, beneficial change is the purpose of democratic government: to **"promote the general welfare."**

When humans forsook hunter-gathering and became agricultural they assumed a measure of control over nature——they altered the environment to improve their circumstance; to enhance their survival by providing a more reliable supply of food; and less wandering allowed them to build more permanent and secure and larger settlements. In changing their relationship to the environment additional human traits were offered for selection, and some existing traits exposed to extinction.

"The stability of cultural transmission can be enhanced through conformity (i.e., a disproportionate tendency to adopt the most common behaviour)...This stability allows cultural traits to be maintained...*generating a 'cultural inertia' that can hinder adaptation to changing environmental conditions...*

Through eliciting change in behaviour, often across an entire population, culture can transform the social environment …Culture provides a highly flexible means to adjust to novel conditions and *modify selection*…[a] confusing feature of culture is that it can both speed up and *slow down genetic evolution*…

Culture provides a form of inheritance that is additional to genes and our review indicates it is far from trivial in its consequences for genetic evolution; moreover, the two inheritance streams can interact to influence each other's evolution." (https://www.nature.com/articles/s41467-019-10293-y) (Emphasis added).

Our genetic inheritance carries fear memories from primitive human experiences that no longer need to exist. We are emotionally blocked from making morally rational alterations to the social environment that would lessen the reinforcement of fear driven behaviors and beliefs—self-destructive competitions and conflicts. *The human predicament lies in unconscious emotions that override rationality.*

A propitious cultural evolution is what the conservative brain obstructs... the conservative amygdala's perception of change as fearful.

....

Through eons of time natural selection has formed its inhabitants to fit the environment. The earliest Homo sapiens had also been formed through adaptation to their natural surroundings, but their descendants would learn to alter the environment; or they would migrate in search of a more favorable environment. And they would develop social relationships that would in turn select and reinforce the social traits that would determine who they would become.

But who would they be? More importantly, who would we be now? For the environment we make will make us. Will we choose social arrangements that relieve our fears and release our innate possibilities, and thereby find our true freedom... and a more sanguine humanity? Or will we remain in selfish, competitive, personal and national conflicts driven by primal emotions... and continue to call that "freedom"... retaining institutions and ideological preferences that deny the realization of our proclaimed principles and human rights? And will we alter our relationship to the environment in ways that invite a promising and plentiful evolution, or hasten our extinction? Or, will the fear of change forever preclude our ability to change... the reactionary brain destined to eternally fall short of possibility... even the possibility of survival?

Evolution offers an intriguing speculation about the anti-social/pro-social brain divide: There was a time about 6 million years ago when the evolutionary lineage that would become Homo sapiens genetically separated from the chimpanzees and bonobos. A few million years later the chimpanzees and bonobos separated from each other. The chimpanzees are noted for competitiveness, aggression, violence and male domination; bonobos are peaceful, cooperative, and female friendly. The anti-social/pro-social conflict was thus present in the common ancestor of all three species prior to genetic separation; and, unfortunately, continued into the Homo sapiens' branch. The chimpanzee and bonobo branches represent a separation of anti-social and pro-social temperaments—two sets of traits exhibiting an internal conflict within a common ancestor dividing into separate species—a process called speciation. The explanation is environmental selection: the bonobos and chimpanzees are geographically separated by the Congo River. The chimpanzees experienced competition with gorillas; the bonobos did not—a more sanguine environment made a more sanguine creature. Greater competition for survival selects greater selfishness and aggression, which is then transmitted through natural selection and cultural conditioning. And that is what humans are doing. We should follow the bonobos.

Will humans eventually resolve their conflict between selfishness (id) and benevolence (superego) by dividing into anti-social and pro-social species: chimpanzee humans and bonobo humans living in separated worlds? Is the id and superego dichotomy inherent in human nature—genetically prescribed brain structures, or is it the result of environmental and cultural conditioning? Is America's ethos of competition for wealth and power assuring the ascendency of Freud's id to the throne once held by democracy's promise? Are the chimps winning?

So, think about this: neuroscience research has shown that female tears contain a chemical that diminishes male aggression by lowering testosterone levels; evolution selected a mutation that aided female survival in the face of aggressive male domination—tearful submission for survival tells much about the history and present of Homo sapiens gender relations. The primitive natural environment imposed (selected) an aggressive, moral insensibility on the male brain that the social environments of succeeding "civilizations" have only somewhat alleviated. It is not difficult to understand why: the male hunter-warrior mentality (violent proclivity, suppressed emotive sympathy, dominance seeking, competitive fervor, *neoliberal greed*) has been reinforced by 300,000 years of natural selection—the best spear throwers survived. The average male has half the humanitarian sensibility of a female. Through endless male violence, driven by survival fears, the specie has survived through female caregiving. Humanity would have seen much less violence in its stumbling history if women had been the principal determiners of governance. A great portion of Homo sapiens masculinum is lagging.

After a long evolution of mutation and selection humankind has a brain *presumably* capable of rational choice. If we want to be a peaceful and benevolent life-form venturing toward the possibilities of cognitive and emotional evolution, then we must make a social environment that allows us to get there. Encouraging and rewarding the gravitational greed of selfishness—the neoliberal relentless pulling of benefit to itself—is the path of continuing social discord, of individual and tribal conflicts, not a benevolent and progressing harmony. We must see what character and behavior human culture is currently rewarding. It is not virtue that is selected by the neoliberal environment—it is selfishness, greed and corruptibility. We appeal to the "better angels" of our nature—is our social environment selecting angels?

Evolutionary adaptation was a concession to *natural* reality, it was not approval of reality. So why not make a *social* reality to which we can approvingly adapt? It will be a hard journey for the human brain is far more capable of madness than sublimity; far more eager for self-indulgence in the moment, than self-transcendence for the future. Will the evolutionary end of human history be a culmination of enlightenments and transcendent achievements? Or will it be a slow, bewildering, determined self-termination by unresolvable conflict—the selfish and humanitarian brains battling on until evolution decides?

And thus, began politics... the fight over preferred social habitat: different levels of primal fear and greed each desiring its preferred conditions and opportunities, the social arrangements and tribal identities that most secure and satisfy the subjective self.

....

This hypothesis has attempted to describe what humankind has largely become: a brain formed and ruled by the emotions of primal fear; a brain exhibiting a defensive and often violent selfishness in response to environmental events that were signs of threat to primitive humans—predators, different others, unfamiliar situations, strangers in the forest—resulting in a conservative reactionary politics seeking and defending personal and tribal advantage, and opposing social liberalism's advancement of human liberty, equality and security. It is the politics of the sociopath, of a brain *absent empathic sensibilities and humanitarian principles*, striving for power and control through membership in the class and factions that insist on a "freedom" for selfish ambitions to achieve economic and political dominance; and the repression of others to maintain that dominance. It is a fearful brain opposing change as a threat to its comforting environment... its social advantages, and reassuring and self-justifying beliefs. The political divide is a neurological divide between more fearful and less fearful brains—brain structural and functional differences that are initially determined by genetic levels of fear (amygdala reactivity) expressed through emotional and behavioral responses; which are then reinforced or moderated by the cultural environment. In American politics, the ungenerous, defensively entrenched brain, insistent on advantage for me and mine, and resistant to equality for all, is generally called Republican.

There is a neuroscientific basis for the political divide underlying all human cultures: *the conservative brain reveals an enlarged amygdala in functional MRI imaging; the liberal brain shows more gray matter in the prefrontal cognitive region.* The supposition of this hypothesis is that increased amygdala volume translates into increased sensitivity to environmental sensory information perceived as threat, resulting in increased self-protective beliefs and behaviors—beliefs that invent reassuring subjective realities; behaviors that pursue social advantage—political power and economic wealth... the visible ambitions of insatiable greed and the arrogant indifference to the plight of others.

On the other side, the enlarged neural volume of the prefrontal cortex suggests greater cognitive capacity for principle and reason, respect for factual reality, and control of fear emotions; allowing for an expanded understanding and appreciation for truth and justice, and desire for the alleviation of human conflict and suffering... the looming "do-gooder" so foreign and threatening to the conservative's morally bereft sensibility. The conservative brain does not merely resist justice and equality because they require changes and uncertainties that arouse the amygdala's fear, it *pursues* unjust and unequal advantages as refuge.

When a brain is faced with a changing environment it has three options: It can consciously adapt by altering its beliefs and behavior to harmoniously perform in the new reality. Or, it can attempt to forestall the change through obstructive resistance. Or, thirdly, it can flounder between transforming itself or preventing change; and unhappily submit to the stresses of undesirable circumstances.

....

Here is what Hayek had to say about conservatives:

"I doubt whether there can be such a thing as a conservative political philosophy…it does not give us any guiding principles which can influence long-range developments."

"…one of the fundamental traits of the conservative attitude is a fear of change, a timid distrust of the new as such..."

"…the conservatives are inclined to use the powers of government to prevent change or to limit its rate to whatever appeals to the more timid mind."

"…the conservative does not object to coercion or arbitrary power so long as it is used for what he regards as the right purposes." (i.e., authoritarian, not democratic).

"...the conservative inclines to defend a particular established hierarchy and wishes authority to protect the status of those whom he values..." (i.e., authoritarian, not democratic).

"...Conservatives fear new ideas because it has no distinctive principles of its own to oppose to them... conservatism is bound by the stock of ideas inherited" (F.A. Hayek; *Why I Am Not a Conservative,* 1960) (parentheses added).

The conservative is on the side of human inequality because he lacks the courage for equality, not because any true principle calls for it. He calls inequality "meritocracy" to assure himself he deserves the privilege and advantage he enjoys. An insightful exposure of conservative "principles" would be a listing of the unprincipled wrongs they are conserving... and refusing to rectify. The allegiance to tradition as "the wisdom of the past" conserves the wrongs of the past; and betrays a lack of vision and moral impulse for improvements. Opposing change is not so much an embrace of "tradition" as an embrace of familiarity against the threat of change and uncertainty. Fear is the strongest and oldest emotion, a brain formed by it is not amenable to sympathetic and generous sentiments for relieving the suffering of others; the psychological opposition to change cannot afford concessions to the demand for justice, for that would mean a return to fear. The conservative is not so fond of the past as he is fearful of changing the present. Conservative obstructions are aided by the humanitarian's good faith brain that is so often naive to the existence of bad faith.

How men have lived—and do live—is a product of previous natural selections and prior cultural conditioning. Human possibility is not confined to the pathways of history; only fear of the light keeps men huddled in the darkness of conflict—the essence of the reactionary brain's cling to the "wisdom" of the past… and the *injustice* of the past. It is a defense of superiority to fortify security that only results in continuing enmity… and insecurity.

(Resistance to change relates directly to brain function: "Plasticity" refers to the ability of the brain to adapt to changing information. *When the information pathway from higher order brain areas is impaired behavioral flexibility is lost.* Conservative opposition to change may be a functional inability of the brain to process new information to overcome prior learning and early life conditioning. Without neural plasticity the human brain is a captive of its first tribal lessons; conflicting facts, truth, and moral aspirations must be denied).

In the 18th century the classical liberals began the overthrow of aristocracy by replacing the hereditary aristocrats with commercial aristocrats. Then those economic "liberals" became political conservatives... once having established they would then conserve the wealth aristocracy. Turns out The Age of Revolution that waved the banner of "freedom" did not have human equality in mind, only new occupants in the privileged places. *Democracy and equality were useful predicates, but not desired ends*

....

The conservative's primal fear of difference and unfamiliarity makes him opposed to the equality of others: why allow your threats to be equal? On first thought, the logic may seem sound; though the psychology paranoid and the politics anti-democratic. On second thought, making the other an enemy intensifies the threat; verifying and deepening the paranoia and reinforcing the fear. The brain of a fearful prey animal has become a fearful predator— defensive fear has become offensive fear—imagining, thus creating its enemies, constructing fortresses, and manufacturing tools of destruction... *the fearful brain is too afraid to alter the conditions that perpetuate its fears.*

And on further thought, how could the conservative brain, resistant to change, survive the ages when adaptability is requisite for long-term survival (Perhaps the ultimate irony!), unless dragged along by those more courageously adaptable? The conservative seeks to prevent change in the habitat that would require his adaptation; the progressive seeks changes in habitat that would support the selection of humanitarian traits. Progress is made by not being overly dependent on the familiar... and being open to possibility.

The politics of fear easily recruits and manipulates through demagoguery and fear mongering and scapegoating and repetitive lies and deceiving assertions (**"government is the problem"**), the emotionally driven, cognitively impaired credulity of others to believe false realities; and to support social policies contrary to their own material interests—the lower-class paradox of supporting the privilege and advantage of "superiors." Being mired in absence of thoughtful examination leaves the bewildered mind vulnerable to the simplest appearance of certainty— the ranting demagogue blaming others and promising deliverance. *The more fearful the brain the more responsive it is to promises of salvation.*

Thus, the uninformed brain, even when disadvantaged, will defend the cultural habitat to which it is conformed, the fear of change and the "safety" of familiarity overriding any consciousness of inferior status. *The demagogue promises to save the familiar and defeat the unfamiliar.* It is also why the aged tend to conservatism—feelings of vulnerability bring fear to the surface when life-long, reassuring familiarities are threatened.

In a neoliberal world of selfish deceits and competitions for advantage it can be a mistake to accept advertisements and appearances as an assurance of reality. A world in which verification needs to be the protector of trust speaks for itself. It is the dissolving world we live in: *the false but appealing promise of the lie will always have a more attentive audience than the sometimes uncomfortable reality of the Truth.*

It could be otherwise: changing the social environment would provide an opportunity to construct institutional conditions that reinforce the emotional and behavioral traits that would make a better world; conditions that lessen the effects of fear and insecurity upon a child's developing brain; conditions that enhance the development of all people for the betterment of the whole community. The choice for humanity is clear: shall humans cooperate for the security and fulfillment of all their lives, or continue to fight over preeminence for a few? Human society needs nothing more than social conditions that favor the angel and impede the reptile.

"Egoistic impulses are so much more powerful than altruistic ones...The justice which even good men design is partial to those who design it." (Reinhold Niebuhr; *Moral Man and Immoral Society*, 1932).

And therein lies the evolutionary struggle: the more recently evolved cortex, informed by self-evident Truths, is having great difficulty in overcoming the unevolved reptilian brain, still conditioned and confined by primal emotions, defending institutions of social competition and hierarchy that do not relieve, but continue to excite and reinforce its fears. It is not obvious that it ever will... the unrestrained ferocity of reptiles is not easily subdued by the moral self-restraints of angels. History tells us that much.

A mutation came along and galvanized the early human brain into a rapid and vast expansion of complexity and rational capacity, leaving the primal brain lagging behind. But that cortex is yet to escape the jaws of the reptile, leaving human character stranded in merciless dichotomies between Good and Evil, Right and Wrong, Vice and Virtue—and the dueling, siren calls of id and superego.

Politics, then, is a primal conflict over defending or transforming the social habitat. Transformation is the difficult task... as every reformer knows. Culture indoctrinates the human brain to its present reality; social change requires breaking through the mental structures of previous conditioning... and compliant brains greatly outnumber brains capable of critical reflections and visions of more "perfect unions." The conservative only needs to arouse the innate fear of change and uncertainty, and the threat of strangers pounding on the castle door; the progressive must calm the fear and reveal the possibility of an improved life—the achievability of our hopes and dreams. The expectation has been that education would introduce a wider world of objective Truths to the subjective spheres of parochial learning. Sadly, brain flexibility is not a universal trait.

But the greatest opportunity for change comes with the devastation of existing conditions through calamity; *when the failure of familiarity itself induces a loss of faith in what has been familiar.* Then a new habitat can be conceived, and a new inhabitant emerge, the shape of the new often implicit in the failure of the old—the phoenix from the ash.

However, the ultimate question remains: how does the human brain, conditioned to its surrounding environment, gather the neural wisdom and courage to alter the social conditions to which it is conformed and psychologically dependent? The suggestion here is *less provocation of primal fear through expanded economic security,* thus less inducement to competition for social advantage; and less dependency on fear relieving beliefs, by being less indoctrinated to narrow cultural attitudes during the most formative years of a child's brain development, when the opportunity for a true freedom to discover the world and oneself is either gained or lost to the preconceptions of our "caregivers". That means a basic economic security, and a system of education independent of political and religious and cultural preconditioning, accountable only to truth and reason… therein lies the chance of true freedom.

A better world has not been found by selfishness in pursuit of happiness; there is a chance it may be found by compassion in the pursuit of equality and justice… and the desire to learn prevailing over the passion for amusement… and the dismantlement of class societies.

Species become stressed when their traits are no longer advantaged and they are incapable or unwilling to adapt to a changing environment. *Inadaptability is a certain evolutionary path to extinction.* **"Created equal"** was and is an existential threat to the selfish brain; hence, the bottomless bad faith deceits of the conservative reaction... and the bitter divide between the forces of change and resistance. So, yes, politics is a primal struggle... and it will decide the human character that sways the interim; ultimately, it is evolution's decision—the ultimate power of Nature to determine beginnings and endings.

Only a virtuous soul can lead to a virtuous world. Otherwise, politics is a conflict won by the strongest... stronger in coercive force or voting numbers. The social habitat must at least allow, if not encourage the rise of virtue. Neoliberal culture (unregulated economic competition for individual survival) gives harbor and favor to the ambitions of the unvirtuous soul—the absence of moral conscience; the absence of remorse in the emotional workings of the selfish brain.

. . . .

From the beginning America was not a *democratic* republic—to be represented in government was the privilege of propertied white men. America remains a republic dominated by private wealth. The enduring honor of America's Founders, however, is that whatever their personal motives, they wrote words that stood in judgment even of themselves. Their words stand in judgment of every generation—*words have implications that are not restricted by intentions*. A people's democracy was the Revolution's promise; its achievement still waits before us... America is not *yet* America.

"...the manufacturing aristocracy which is growing up under our eyes is one of the harshest which ever existed...the friends of democracy should keep their eyes anxiously fixed in this direction, for if ever a *permanent inequality* of conditions and aristocracy again penetrate into the world, it may be predicted that this is the gate by which they will enter." (Tocqueville; *Democracy in America,* 1835-40; book 2, Ch.34, last paragraph) (Emphasis added).

Tocqueville's concluding thought, in the last paragraph of his multi-year study of democracy in America, was that the commercial pursuit of private wealth would destroy American democracy—*unless democracy had vigilant friends*.

"We find our population suffering from old inequalities, little changed by past sporadic remedies. In spite of our efforts and in spite of our talk we have not weeded out the over privileged and we have not effectively lifted up the under privileged... Americans must forswear that conception of the acquisition of wealth which, through excessive profits, creates undue private power over... public affairs...A decent living throughout life is an ambition to be preferred to the appetite for great wealth and great power." (Franklin Roosevelt; *State of The Union,* 1935).

As we now know, Tocqueville and FDR were prescient; private wealth and its unregulated freedom, have become the new hereditary aristocracy; a burgeoning *transnational*, corrupt and tax evading ***"permanent inequality."*** A government by the people and for the people is now a government for those who can afford to buy it.

. . . .

The Declaration of Independence is an American document only in the sense of its first application. In word and spirit, it is a human document, a universal declaration of the unalienable rights and equality of all women and men and children everywhere.

"The cause of America is in a great measure the cause of all mankind." (Thomas Paine; *Common Sense*, January 10, 1776).

The virtuous men have mostly acceded to the men of selfish interest—want has defeated ought; fear and greed are more intense and determined than good-will and generosity; the ambitions of avarice readily trample the self-restraints of virtue.

Virtue is an inescapable feeling of obligation; the obedience of conscience to principles of Right and Good that are greater than the reptilian impulses that lurk within ourselves. True freedom—and true individualism—requires overcoming the primal ghost and standing up the virtuous self; the final triumph of the evolved cortex over the emotions of primal fear. Freedom is not unrestraint of the animal spirit; it is the power of mind to impose what is Right and Good upon itself; the power of an evolved conscience over the primal compulsions of fear.

Are we, then, but self-preserving reptiles bellowing our egoistic wants, or are we patriot angels with Enlightenment virtues... striving to do what we ought... ever knowing that the good we intend never excuses the harms we accomplish?

Has virtue really died?
Or did it never truly live?
Perhaps it was only briefly tried...
Then forsaken for a bribe.

"These communities, by their representatives in old Independence Hall, said to the whole world of men: 'We hold these truths to be self-evident: that all men are created equal; that they are endowed by their Creator with certain unalienable rights; that among these are life, liberty and the pursuit of happiness." This was their majestic interpretation of the economy of the Universe. This was their lofty, and wise, and noble understanding of the justice of the Creator to His creatures. Yes, gentlemen, to all His creatures, to the whole great family of man. In their enlightened belief, nothing stamped with the Divine image and likeness was sent into the world to be trodden on, and degraded, and imbruted by its fellows. They grasped not only the whole race of man then living, but they reached forward and seized upon the farthest posterity. They erected a beacon to guide their children and their children's children, and the countless myriads who should inhabit the earth in other ages. Wise statesmen as they were, they knew the

tendency of prosperity to breed tyrants, and so they established these great self-evident truths, that when in the distant future some man, some faction, some interest, should set up the doctrine that none but rich men, or none but white men, were entitled to life, liberty and the pursuit of happiness, their posterity might look up again to the Declaration of Independence and take courage to renew the battle which their fathers began---so that truth, and justice, and mercy, and all the humane and Christian virtues might not be extinguished from the land; so that no man would hereafter dare to limit and circumscribe the great principles on which the temple of liberty was being built...

Now, my countrymen, if you have been taught doctrines conflicting with the great landmarks of the Declaration of Independence; if you have listened to suggestions which would take away from its grandeur, and mutilate the fair symmetry of its proportions; if you have been inclined to believe that all men are not created equal in those inalienable rights enumerated by our chart of liberty, let me entreat you to come back. Return to the fountain whose waters spring close by the blood of the Revolution...come back to the truths that are in the Declaration of Independence." (Abraham Lincoln, August 17, 1858; Lewistown, Illinois).

....

The fact that the historical push for justice is always opposed by hatred and violence and distrust does not invalidate the rightness of justice; nor lessen the moral duty to pursue it. The fierce opposition to justice reveals the depth of the fear that opposes it. Abidance of injustice because its advocates are so determined, because they are so psychologically dependent on superiority is to sacrifice the possibility of a better world.

Democracy's ideals are not impossibilities; it is the reality of now that declines to achieve the possible... so far. We are early in Homo sapiens evolution; we may reasonably expect the neocortex to eventually overrule the amygdala's primal fears; though expectation does not mean patiently waiting for evolution to mutate us into an enlightened state of mind, it means pushing the process of selection by changing the modes of survival—like making benevolence more profitable than selfishness. Hence, politics.

Only we must believe that the current condition of human belief and behavior does not define the fullness of our nature; that our dreams of possibility are not restricted by our current circumstance. We have to live in reality as we find it in the moment; we do not have to accept it as our future. The reality we now face was made by those who preceded us; it is our right to judge it, and change it; it is not a prescription to be obeyed; it is a presentation to be accepted, or not.

The search for Truth requires a reach that sometimes finds mistake, but the reach is imperative, for we must know the truth or live by lies and fallacies. And to accept the lie is to sacrifice the dream.

Whither is fled the visionary gleam?
Where is it now, the glory and the dream?

(William Wordsworth; *Ode: Intimations...*)

Community salvation will require the heart and mind of a whole people to find a common voice, and speak their own prophesy for the renewal of democracy, and the emancipation of the better angel. It should begin in America, where the cry for common liberty was raised by a common man—common in his beginnings, foremost in his destiny.

"We have it in our power to begin the world over again." (Thomas Paine; *Common Sense*, January 1776).

"Without the pen of the author of Common Sense, the sword of Washington would have been raised in vain." (John Adams).

PART TWO

THE AMYGDALA HYPOTHESIS

We have come from fear,
From dark forests with danger ever near.
We ventured upon the open plain,
Each step a trembling suspicious stride.
Was it courage that brought us from the foliage,
Or had the plains become a lesser fear?
Now timorous steps have found their way,
The fearful brain has taken sway.
For all the fear so long endured,
The world will now and ever pay.

CHAPTER ONE

Amygdala's Memory:
A Heritage of Fear

The three great facts of life are its occurrence, its persistence, and its evolution. The force that enters into life, from the single-celled organism to the wise hominin, seeks to thrive and become, and for this determined journey it must survive. To survive in life requires avoiding the dangers that would end it. To be avoided, these dangers must be sensed by an innate awareness. This innate awareness is the amygdala's memories of fear—the evolutionary recording of what has threatened survival in the past. Among these recorded threats are known predators, and sudden or unfamiliar changes in the environment.

The amygdala (ah-MIG-dah-la) is an organ of the primitive, or reptilian, brain. The primitive brain is also called reptilian because it dates from the time of the great reptiles. It is this primitive part of the brain that controls the survival functions and reflexes of vertebral life forms. Hundreds of millions of years old, the amygdala remains the center of the human brain's survival system. It signals other regions of the brain when it detects sensory inputs from the environment that represent threats to survival.

In addition to avoidance of danger the amygdala is also central to pleasure seeking behavior. Evolutionary survival is not only about avoiding existential threat, but also obtaining nourishment and satisfying needs. Survival is about learning the behavior responses that most reliably achieve the goal—how to escape or conquer threat, how to hunt for food and find shelter from exposure, and how to obtain a mate. This hypothesis, however, is concerned with the fear-based response and will not address pleasure seeking or hunting/stalking behavior, except to note that an overly reactive amygdala in the pursuit of pleasure and dominance and satisfaction of need may be as destructive to self and others—addictions, sexual predation, greed—as the excessive fear response. As well, it seems obvious that a behavior that escapes danger is likely to be very gratifying; and that it will be reinforced not only by its success in relieving the fear emotion, but also by the pleasure and satisfaction of accomplishment—as in escaping or suppressing the social threat of competitors through economic and political domination... or even by harmful aggression. Whatever makes the emotional brain happy (dopamine release), whether good or evil, will be learned, remembered and repeated—becoming conditioned beliefs and behaviors. Nature accomplishes its survival imperative by making dangerous things fearful and advantageous things pleasurable. The amygdala is involved in both. And we will see, whether behavior is evil or good depends on other brain functions being able to moderate behavioral responses to the amygdala's alarm.

As the infant brain enters the birth environment it begins a learning process through an initial sense of comfort or discomfort with its surroundings… whether to smile or cry. The new brain is in a process of adaptation to the conditions in which it must survive; it must learn to assess where it is and what it must do. The five senses will provide information about the environment which the amygdala will monitor for signs of danger—like a motion detector sensing movement—and secondarily, to detect opportunity for satisfaction or enjoyment or enhancement. The brain is a hazard/benefit sensing device. It is busily informing itself to discover successful responses to significant stimuli, and then remembering the result to establish reliable approach or avoidance behaviors; conditioned responses that avoid the potentially dangerous delay of having to analyze every call to action. But here's the curious part: the conscious "self" is not doing this; the brain machine is doing it. Consciousness seems to emerge from brain activity the way a rainbow appears through the interaction of sunlight and water droplets, as a consequence of interacting neurological events, not as a cause of the events. "I" am not telling my neurons what to do. This non-causal, lagging emergence of conscious awareness raises questions about who or what is in charge; questions about freewill and self-determination; about freedom and individualism; about achievement and personal merit.

Fully functioning by age three, the amygdala easily dominates the still developing prefrontal cortex, which does not near full development until around age 25. The frontal cortex is the forward part of the cerebral cortex which is intended to eventually exercise rational control over the amygdala's emotional impulses. We are, however evolved we imagine ourselves to be, captives to our reptilian survival impulses. That is, until, and if, the frontal cortex learns to moderate our primal reflexes with more considered responses. As noted in Part One:

"The more recently evolved components of the nervous system depend on the function of more ancient systems. Neocortical structures are in general subservient to systems necessary for survival. More primitive systems and behaviors, including those associated with fear and anxiety, may inhibit positive social behaviors and cognitive strategies." (ibid.) (Emphases added).

The problem is we have no considered responses at birth. The prefrontal cortex, by which we hope to live a reasoned life, is incipient, unprepared to evaluate the amygdala's alarms. And alarms there are, for birth clearly presents sudden and startling sensations to the infant brain, which begin when the encapsulating security of the amniotic sac breaks, and the emergent organism is alerted to imminent change, which quickly becomes expulsion into unfamiliar surroundings. Sudden change and separation into an unfamiliar environment, and a cascade of novel sensations provide the initial alarms to the amygdala—and they will remain signs of possible threat for the life of the organism. And critically, it is the degree of the amygdala's genetic reactivity to environmental stimuli that will greatly influence the individual's developing brain, mental health, personality, social behavior, political opinions and tribal identity.

Birth is a stressful disruption of the calm and ordered process of creation, from the comfort and security of oneness into the discomfort and insecurity of separation. Gradually, over the early months and first years of life, awareness builds that well-being is not automatic—that there is no umbilical cord streaming with life's satisfactions; that our needs and satisfactions depend on something outside of, and apart from, our self; that we must cry and scream our fears and displeasure. Only immediate accommodation, physical and emotional bonding to an affectionate primary caregiver who can moderate the transformation from fetal to birth environment, from oneness to separation, can hope to calm the amygdala. That we are born to a world not always eager to satisfy our needs is the primal conclusion of the amygdala dominated incipient brain.

As this newly arrived infant brain is being formed by genetic instruction—neurons marching to their prescribed destinations—it will also be influenced by its experience of the new environment, adapting its neural formations and connections in response to external signals… experience is dictating the brain's architecture and installing cultural and tribal beliefs, which are credible and determining because the prefrontal cortex is in the process of forming and lacks the functional independence, the logical and critical capability, and even the conscious awareness to mediate them. The infant brain cannot reject or alter its environment.

And so, before the brain/mind ever gains some selective control of its experiences it is formed by them—whoever it is that we are becoming, it is not by our choices.

The survival imperative compels adaptation to the environment or alteration of the environment—submission and conformance; or eventually, if early indoctrination is overcome, contention or rebellion.

The birth environment thus begins its cultural branding, indoctrinating the brain to the surrounding beliefs and behaviors. We are made to fit the clan, to share its customs and myths. Nonconformity and dissent are destabilizing, a threat to unifying, self-justifying, and fear-relieving beliefs; especially non-evidenced beliefs that depend on unquestioned adherence... and which are also a threat to the interests of tribal authorities demanding unquestioned loyalty. The incentive to conform is the safety and comfort of acceptance and belonging, and the fear of banishment. Few individuals survive early indoctrination to develop independent minds and see the clan's "truth" as arbitrary—true freedom is more easily found by a non-indoctrinated beginning. The brain that eventually emerges is a mixture of genetic inheritance and submission to cultural and environmental persuasions—an amalgam of nature, nurture and cultural influences. A truly free human person may be a somewhat rare and solitary thing.

It is experience that tells the developing brain which neurons to keep and which to shed—the neural connections stimulated by the environment are strengthened, while those not stimulated are weakened and gradually discarded (synaptic pruning). This is a key fact underlying why early conditioning and indoctrination impose cultural content that can be so limiting and indelible, as experience structures the brain and thus its function and behavioral expression. The birth environment is a cultural potter's wheel, shaping the infant brain—chromosomes provide the clay, experience shapes the bowl. Thus, the first experiences of life are critical—the earlier and longer that a hyperactive amygdala's danger messages are imposed upon the incipient cortex the stronger will be the neural formation of fear-based belief and behavior patterns, and weaker will be the supervision of rational and moral restraints—egocentric behavior will be strengthened, obligation to principle and the larger community diminished. With the synapses that are pruned goes parts of who we might have been. In the case of what is called "amygdala hijack," a hyperactive amygdala enlists the compliance of an incipient cortex with the amygdala's reality—the cognitive brain then becomes not the moral regulator of our fear-based behaviors, but the rationalizer seeking to justify.

Creation thus occurs with a genetic intent, but experience will alter it. Experience can serve to nurture and realize neurological inheritance, or repress and limit it (This fact is of great importance for infant parenting and early pre-school education. How many of us as young parents understand the developmental requirements of the infant brain... especially how our attending moods and attitudes convey, or not, the assurance of safety and loving and supportive attachment?). Forty-six chromosomes are molded by the birth environment into an inner self that will one day emerge into a larger reality, whence we come to further know ourselves as others experience and relate to us, telling us who we are—an unchosen self that we must make the best of, or not.

In all the important things, then, the human brain is far more determined than we want to believe; "free-will" seems a minor, if not absent, participant. Beyond the initial genetic dictates, at birth we enter a forming process. The brain is "learning" about its environment long before "we" are aware of it. There is no "will" or "choice", no self-determination. There is no point in the brain's early development when saint or sociopath, angel or reptile, is a conscious choice. We are immersed in a sea of stimuli, subject to the amygdala's emotional dictates, compelled by unconscious neurological events. To believe that everyone has chosen consciously and knowingly, and with freedom of will, the lives they are living, is a thoroughly mistaken belief.

We begin, then, as possibility and immediately succumb to vulnerability, open to the accumulating effects and assaults of cascading sensations, and the commissions and omissions of our caregivers. Emotional neglect of children, the absence of affectionate attention and time-sharing interaction that builds emotional security and a sense of self-worth, is commonplace in a competitive society of stressed and striving parents. Our fate is largely found in our beginning moments, whether our introduction to life occurs in a garden of love and security and positive stimulation or a chamber of physical and emotional harms and privations. Even a mother's prenatal stress level has negative effects on the fetal brain. We have not chosen ourselves any more than the oceans have chosen the tides.

And therein lies life's fundamental unfairness: We do not make ourselves and thus we are not to be blamed for who we are, but we must be responsible nonetheless. For who else carries the inheritance of genes and environmental effects but ourselves? Would it not be a greater unfairness that others bear responsibility for the consequences of our agency? Human agency is more an effect of biological and environmental happenstance than conscious choices. Wrongdoing can only be stopped by restricting the freedom of the agents who do it... and of those who suborn it. Society's first duty is the protection of innocence. The social question is what behaviors are to be considered a violation of innocence. *Non-abuse of others is the undeniable limiting principle upon freedom.*

The true meaning of freedom and individuality may only be measured by the extent we are able to overcome the thoughts and behaviors that have emerged within us. Conditioned thoughts and habitual behaviors are not expressions of moral freedom—they represent the experiences and prejudices that have informed us. There is no freedom in having been determined.

Because of less than perfect childhood environments almost all of us are less than what we might have been; and many have been severely robbed of their genetic possibilities. And then those less hindered by their beginning circumstances think themselves superior, and more deserving of the possibilities of life. Having been given the gift of being less robbed they think it achievement.

Perhaps Homo sapiens is the apex of creation, though our view into the cosmos is too brief and short in time and distance to ever know. Whatever, to be a life-form so favored by the elements with self-consciousness and the appearance of intelligence, and placed in such a beautiful and habitable world, is it too much to suppose that we can improve ourselves? And be less fearful of the changes required.

Implied in all this is another possibility. An amygdala less biochemically reactive to environmental signs of threat or pleasure, and/or more emotionally secured by first experiences, would send fewer and more moderate alarms, thus allowing neural activity to develop toward a more balanced state of mind. This balanced mind would likely learn to perceive the world with more trust and confidence and consideration for others, less fear and suspicion, less selfishness, and less defensive aggression—it would reflect and return the goodness it has received. And it would be less dependent on controlled surroundings, thus more open to arguments for change; and less threatened, thus less resistant to the equality of others. It would, in fact, be a more empathetic and cooperative brain... and more amenable to the internal voice of conscience. And if culture would step back and offer a less imposing indoctrination to provincial beliefs and prejudices, a true individuality might find the neurological freedom to emerge into a more self-discovered human person. A childhood of little indoctrination gives the blessing of much to discover and little to overcome.

But there is a downside to having little to overcome when it means growing up naive and uninformed, and having to learn from blind efforts that, however honest and trusting, often lead to painful and costly experiences. Being educated means learning about the universal experiences and possibilities and uncertainties of life; being indoctrinated is being told what to believe and how to behave. The former contributes to practical and cautious wisdom on a path to personal discovery, the latter precludes the discovery by imposing the destination.

So, humans have two brains: the brain whose early development is dominated by excessive amygdala reactions to primal threats; and the brain that develops without the excessive impositions of fear, to achieve cognitive independence and moral regulation of emotional impulses. The cognitive brain seeks to ascertain and understand objective reality. The emotional brain, under the urgency of emotional alarm, cannot wait for understanding or discovery or considered responses, so it adopts invented realities—beliefs that assuage its emotions, and defensive reactions and strategies to counteract perceived threats. The cognitive brain explores for knowledge and seeks to remedy wrongs. The emotional brain reacts against change as a threat to the comforts of familiarity, and against the remedy of wrongs as a threat to advantage, and against Truth as a threat to belief—for belief is essential where knowledge is absent… the unknown may harbor dangers even greater than what is known. And for the fearful brain embracing available beliefs is easier than exploring the unknown, or accepting unanswerable mysteries. But there lies the dilemma: an optimum evolution requires intelligent adaptation, and intelligent adaptation requires Truth about the environment. Those burdened with untrue beliefs go blindly toward the future; and fate does not give consideration to human beliefs or opinions or preferences.

Both brains are evolutionary selections; each have contributed to survival success—the amygdala brain to physical survival, escaping or avoiding danger in the moment; the neocortex to evolutionary advance—from prey animal to ultimate predator, from wandering the savanna to building civilizations. Whether the ultimate outcome is an individualist seeking social domination or a humanitarian refraining from domination depends on brain structure and content—education, memories, beliefs, learned prejudices, as well as the function and connectivity between brain regions; over which the amygdala has such early formative influence.

But there remains a question deep within the brain, a fork in the neural road: would reason assist fear's more selfish inclinations, or guide emotion toward less selfish behaviors? The hypothesis being described here is about the neural strength of the amygdala's emotions commanding prefrontal cortex complicity in pursuit of fear-based motives, rationalizing aggressive beliefs and behaviors in defense against perceived threats, forming the conservative brain. Politics is the battleground between reason as enabler and reason as moral self-restraint—abetting or restraining the freedom of socioeconomic selfishness. The choice of classical liberalism was the freedom of selfishness.

The struggle between the fear emotions and moral reason for control of the prefrontal cortex generally mirrors Freud's id and superego... with ego being the resolution—the compromised personality that emerges into the world.

"Our findings are in line with the idea that a primary impulse in humans may be to help and cooperate, whereas the execution of calculative-instrumental—that is, selfish—behaviors are learned from interactions with the social environment..." (nih.gov).

If social cooperation is man's nature, or at least his inclination, is he being driven out of it by an ideology conceived by a fearful brain to give itself a path to social advantage? Are the "laws" of classical liberal economics not laws, but rationalizations that attempt to justify and ascribe inevitability to the selfish brain—the neoliberal claim that there is no alternative?

As described in Part One, the classical liberal ideology of laissez-faire competition is an organization of society that accommodates, rewards and reinforces the aggressively selfish brain, systemically disadvantaging the cooperative brain. Competitive economic ideology supposes to represent human nature, and to duly reward talent. More accurately, it selects and incites, and gives freedom to aggressive ambitions; fear-driven emotions that manifest as a relentless greed, enlisting the frontal cortex's strategic intelligence. Social evolution is being driven by the incitement and reward of selfishness through "success" at economic competition, selecting selfish traits and discouraging unselfishness.

It is believed that early humans survived through group cooperation, which inspired the development of language and intelligence. Selfish behavior is disruptive to cooperative sentiments—and social cohesion generally—creating a climate of one against all. Competition is a result of the selfish brain's insistence on an opportunity—"freedom"—to achieve an advantage in possessions and power. The purpose of specifying inalienable rights is to limit the freedom of power, public and private. Liberty protects against the freedoms that abuse. Due to its importance, and the widespread synonymous use of the terms, this point about the distinction between freedom and liberty, already emphasized above, cannot be repeated too often. Emphasis on critical points in an argument warrants the annoyance of repeating them.

The human brain is predominately emotional. Emotion is understood as a pre-conscious neural reaction of the brain to sensory information received and assessed by the amygdala as significant to survival or opportunity for enhancement. The intensity of the emotion is determined by the level of the amygdala's genetic reactivity and the proximity and imminence of the stimulus. The amygdala creates an emotion for the purpose of driving a response (behavior) to the stimulus, with primary regard to fears and pleasures—avoiding or confronting stimuli that appear threatening; pursuing and possessing stimuli that promise pleasure and satisfaction—food, rest, shelter, safety, sexual fulfillment. Over time evolution selected mutations that led to a neo-cortex for supervising the emotions and improving the chances of survival through intelligent decision-making; moderating the hyper-reactive emotion and regulating against irrational, self-defeating, and morally unacceptable responses (internal restraint). If reason over emotion did not enhance survival why did it evolve so rapidly? Behavior, then, is a question of how much rationality the prefrontal cortex is able to attain, and whether that rationality is directed by selfish emotions or moral sensibility; whether it is prejudicially conditioned, or educated to think critically and ethically. That is, whether the prefrontal cortex aids the sociopath or the humanitarian.

It may be that the sapiens species within the Homo genus was the physically weakest and required an evolved intelligence to compete and survive, yet it remained burdened with a fear-centered brain. The evolution of intelligence overcame the competitors and predators but did not overcome the amygdala's fear instinct. Friendliness and cooperation would have aided survival within the primary group. But the prey animal fear instinct also biased the brain toward wariness, competition and conflict against other primary groups; hence tribalism and the fearful brain's intense reaction to difference—xenophobia... the ominous others! Thus, survival required the selection of both the prosocial emotions of affection, empathy and generosity within the group, and the anti-social emotions of wariness, competitiveness and aggression outside the group. Hence, the amygdala's signposts for survival: in group familiarity means safety (tribal, racial, national identity), while outside group difference and unfamiliarity means possible threat. And so, the emotional tension between goodness and meanness, empathy and antipathy; the divided soul bequeathed by evolution, and revealed in brain difference... and politics. Yet eventually, the selfish brain will express its wariness of the other even within its own community, as the amygdala's fear sinks into a defensive and competitive individualism, seeking advantage and superiority over its neighbors, with a minimal sense of obligation and attachment.

This is a good time to repeat the point that The Declaration's right to pursue happiness does not logically or morally endorse a "freedom" for the selfish brain to impose socioeconomic inferiority on its neighbors, however happy it would make it. The inalienable rights (liberty) of others are not dependent on acceptance by any one's happiness or freedom. The Declaration asserts that *government's purpose is to secure the inalienable rights of all individuals*, not to promote and protect the freedom of any one individual to encroach upon those rights—inalienable rights have precedence over freedom. Laissez-faire capitalism is the invention of an ambition for private wealth and power that emphasizes individual freedom over the mutual right of others to be substantively equal in society, and thus it is inconsistent with democratic principles, i.e., the unregulated economic freedom that favors the aggrandizement of a few, systematically comes to violate the natural and equal rights of all.

"Government is instituted for the common good; for the protection, safety, prosperity, and happiness of the people; and not for profit, honor, or private interest of any one man, family, or class of men; therefore, the people alone have an incontestable, unalienable, and indefeasible right to institute government; and to reform, alter, or totally change the same, when their protection, safety, prosperity, and happiness require it." (John Adams; *Thoughts on Government*, 1776)

The persistent thesis herein is that the conservative brain is biased by an overly active fear response—reflected in brain structure—toward the negative emotions when confronted with difference and change, the signposts of threat. The less fear-minded brain is biased toward the positive emotions, generalizing the harmony of the primal group to humanity as a whole—humanitarianism. The difference being that change and unfamiliarity do not provoke a fear response in the less fear-formed brain—in fact, the opposite, a curiosity for novelty and new experience, and acceptance of positive change; a willingness to remedy wrongs when they appear. Being less fearful of the external world, the liberal mind is less driven to control it, only wishing to make it more just and equal, thus more secure for everyone. The conservative mind is obsessed with control, wishing to make society more advantageous to itself. Hence, its opposition to measures that advance equality, and efforts to devise anti-democratic restrictions upon voting.

The fear of change leaves the brain committed to an emotional and cognitive dependence on past beliefs and social arrangements—a psychological dependence on familiarity is sublimated into a love for tradition. Defending the past blocks the openness and creativity necessary for current remedies, and impedes curiosity and vision for future possibilities.

Resistance to change is the basis of the political intransigence between conservatives and progressives: the divide over social policy is not about what change, but change versus no change; there is little room for compromise between yes, let's do it, and no, let's not.

"…one of the fundamental traits of the conservative attitude is a fear of change, a timid distrust of the new as such, while the liberal position is based on courage and confidence, on a preparedness to let change run its course even if we cannot predict where it will lead." (F.A. Hayek; *Why I Am Not a Conservative*)

When science warns of climate change the conservative is being twice assaulted; he is being told that his environment is changing and therefore his emotionally reassuring beliefs and conditioned behaviors must change. The open mind seeks evidence and solutions, the fearful mind denies the problem... the ostrich strategy. Adaptability is not the forte of the conservative brain; at least not voluntary adaptability. When it comes to survival, we will all adapt if necessary: *fear of death will overcome fear of change*. It must fairly be said we all wish to maintain a safe and pleasurable habitat. The point here is that the humanitarian wishes to make it safe and pleasurable for all; the conservative, not so much.

The conservative brain exists because there was primitive survival expedience to maintenance of a familiar status quo, and to aggression and violence in its defense. But thoughtless defense against change blocks reason's opportunity to reach for improvement and possibility, prolonging wrongs and inadequacies because they are familiar... and traditional. Thus, there is a dilemma: the brain has evolved greater capacity to be adaptive to change, whereas the conservative brain is emotionally and politically resistant to change—emotion resisting reason—which clearly reveals the bifurcated brain, a primitive emotional brain in contention with an evolved cognitive brain. Which brain dominates distinguishes the xenophobe from the humanitarian; the id from the superego. A distant future Homo sapiens, if open-minded and empathic sentiments can overcome conservative resistance, may find their amygdalae unselected, or at least somewhat atrophied from disuse. We can hope.

It must be stated that the conservatism of principles and values is not the subject of this hypothesis. The subject is sociopathic selfishness that seeks political and economic domination over the community, and thus opposes human equality. That same selfishness, however, finds a home among less personally selfish conservatives whose "principled" hostility toward government regulation and adherence to prescriptive traditions despite the wrongs they transmit, also aids and abets an unjust status quo.

(The liberal and conservative political labels represent what is a neurological distinction, expressed in politics as pro-social, pro-government, pro-reform liberals; and pro-self, anti-government, anti-reform conservatives; each group involving a range from moderate to extreme).

It was The Enlightenment's freedom of human reason that led to the Scientific and Industrial Revolutions, and thus to economic development; discoveries in science, advancements in transportation, communication and technology. The human urge to learn and prosper does not require giving to the selfish brain the rewards of wealth and social advantage. In fact, social inequality imposes educational limitations and financial obstacles on the disadvantaged that preclude their contribution to social and economic advancement.

It is on the point of social advantage that the political liberalism that began with The Enlightenment has failed. It liberated the human brain from Dark Age superstition and subservience to the claims of kings, but it was too accepting of the selfish ambitions of economic liberalism. Laissez-faire does not arrive at democracy, it arrives at plutocracy—rule by a wealthy class. Democratic principles and the rights of man were overshadowed by individual freedom and opportunity. Liberty's rights of all were sacrificed to a freedom destined to serve the desires of a few.

If the prefrontal cortex is neurologically independent and empathetically informed, and somewhat cognizant of evidence-based reality, the amygdala is subdued and behavior becomes controlled, guided by a consideration of what ought to be done rather than a reflexive, selfish response to what is desired. Emotions require subjective gratification—fears mollified, desires satisfied, and beliefs embraced that give internal assurance regardless of external, objective truth. For the negative emotions, feeling better is evidence of "truth." Thus, the amorality of expedience—what is true or good is what works for me. And the prevalence of hypocrisy—the opposite of what worked for me yesterday may work for me today. Reason can serve any purpose the prefrontal cortex is inclined, or neurologically compelled to embrace. And if reason is absent, irrationality becomes master. A brain with much fear and little knowledge is soon filled with superstitions and reassuring beliefs... and enemies. And a brain with much fear and much knowledge is soon filled with authoritarian intentions.

The emotional brain does not stop to consult the prefrontal cortex, the prefrontal has to be there watching and thinking, with the cognitive power to intervene; and informed with principles and values that overrule the selfish proclivity

(Brain studies—fMRI—have shown that challenges to political and religious belief activate the same brain region [amygdala] as fear. This is consistent with the amygdala hypothesis: the prefrontal cortex is rationalizing salvation strategies—positing metaphysical beliefs and pursuing political advantages that alleviate fear. A challenge to our comforting beliefs and social advantages is tantamount to a threat to survival, hence the conservative brain's inclination for denying facts and resisting appeals for social justice. Truth and justice are very threatening to protective beliefs and prejudices and social advantages.)

It is presumable that the evolutionary function of reason is to prevent emotion from being self-destructive; and secondarily, to perceive the usefulness of social cooperation. Reason is an advanced survival mechanism struggling to overcome the evolutionary dominance of the amygdala. It is especially with the negative emotions of fear and hate and greed that reason must do its work in controlling appetites and behaviors. Reason is thus evolutionary progressive when serving to support survival by recommending amiable and cooperative behaviors that remove competitive conflicts. And it is monstrously evil when rationalizing the negative emotions of fear and hate, instigating and approving threatening behaviors that perpetuate the rule of hate and fear and violence, thus working against the security in the social environment necessary for healthy neural development. Behavior is the result of an interface between emotion and reason. Empathy cannot emerge, and human evolution will not reach to a promising future until the fears of the reptilian brain are obviated by a culture that values human security over opportunities for selfish ambitions; a community where persons **"created equal"** are not allowed to be made unequal. Humanity is trapped in a vortex, where fear engenders behaviors that engender more fear—a black hole in the brain where enlightenment disappears. Has evolution reached a paradox? Has it stumbled upon a brain whose internal dynamic is turning progress into regress? A brain whose strategy for survival exacerbates the threats to survival? Has Nature created a creature whose destiny is to destroy itself? Has too much intelligence been given to a brain haunted by primal fears, such that ultimate weapons can be invented and deployed preemptively against any appearance, or illusion, of threat? Talk about being "too smart for one's good!"

Evolution involves instances where an evolved capacity is lost when it falls into disuse because of a changed environment—what was previously selected becomes unselected—like penguins losing the ability of flight. Human fear and the selfish/competitive response continue to dominate the social environment, tending to discourage and limit the reinforcement of empathic and cooperative traits. Might this lead to an eventual loss of the positive emotions that facilitated inter group survival, making Man increasingly an individualistic sociopath—a super predator.

There is contention with views of the amygdala's centrality to the fear response, specifically with the "feeling" of fear. But conscious fear is not the point. The beginning point of the fear response is the amygdala's unconscious detection of external threat… when the pebble hits the pond, spreading waves throughout the brain triggering myriad neurological events that culminate in various physiological, psychological and behavioral responses. The feeling of fear occurs when the prefrontal cortex confirms there is reason to be afraid. The amygdala is the lantern in the steeple warning of danger: "One, if by land, and Two, if by sea." Or, for the conservative brain: One, if it's liberal, and two, if progressive!

It seems much of the exception to the focus on the amygdala's central role in the fear response is simply saying, "It is more complicated than that." For sure, the brain is a complicated biological machine—estimates of 86-100 billion neurons, 100 trillion synapses, 180 functionally distinction brain regions. But the principal question for society is: what is a hyper amygdala's effect on social behavior? And is the effect of excessive amygdala fear on the developing brain what differentiates the anti-government, freedom-of-selfishness conservative brain, from the pro-social justice-for-all humanitarian brain? And is the world's dominant economic ideology systemically reinforcing human conflict by rewarding individual selfishness and dissolving social cohesion and common interest?

The description about the prefrontal cortex mediating the amygdala's response seems to presuppose "free-will." Science is undecided if there is such a thing. It is possible that what we experience as conscious choice is simply an observer's awareness of what has already happened in the brain. Has the brain reached a neurological conclusion micro-seconds before conscious awareness thinks it has decided? The brain machine decides and we take credit for better; or responsibility for worse? That "I" am aware of my brain's decision does not mean that I made the decision, no more than my nighttime dream was written and directed by "me." Awareness does not imply cause or control, only witness. In the case of fear, survival required a faster response than considered thought could provide. The brain reacts to a stimulus with an emotional reflex, which initiates a systemic response, a chain of electrical and chemical transmissions not initiated by "me." The brain does not wait for "me" to decide. Does it not also, then, decide on all "appropriate" behaviors based on stored memories, beliefs and habits? Am "I" only a belatedly informed witness giving sometimes flawed testimony to myself about what I think I am doing? Does my brain tell my legs to run, and then I merely come to realize that I am running, and then surmise a reason? Am I deciding to be selfish? Or am I being compelled by my amygdala's hyperactivity and previously conditioned responses, and inadequate moral supervision?

And what of humanity collectively, or at least a controlling majority? If we had a collective free-will, would we not choose against violence and destruction? Against warfare? Does the fact that we don't mean that we can't?

There is another point that regards free-will. It has to do with the bootstrap theory. The conservative is inclined to blame inequality on the "losers"—they don't try hard enough; they have an "equal opportunity" but they're too lazy or stupid to use it; they fail because of lack of character, absence of work ethic. The problem is these judgments are too simplistic, and the judges too ignorant or too dismissive of the genetic and environmental factors that benefit or impair mental ability; and also, that competitive games necessarily have many more losers than winners. So maybe the stupid part is being unaware of the complex causation that underlies the development of human capacity—and expecting competition to have no losers. The ultimate stupid part, or rather malevolent part, is the imposition of debilitating living conditions on others and then blaming them for being debilitated.

The opposite error would be to say there is no personal responsibility—of course there is. But the truth is there is no equal beginning or equal opportunity. How we start out and how we are aided by genetic talents and human mentors, or hindered by obstructions and discouragements is not our doing. If we all had a "free-will" most of us would choose to be other than we are. After considering the brain's susceptibility to environmental affects there really is more in our stars than ourselves. So, is blaming the loser just being simplistic, or is it another way of saying, "I do not care?

Consider the conservative mentality: adherence to prescriptive traditions because familiarity is comforting; resistance to equality because advantage is, well, an advantage; hostility to science because knowledge threatens reassuring *or useful* beliefs—and may require change. Change, threats to advantage, difference—a strange face living next door—all provoke the emotions of fear and selfish strategies of defense… the reptilian brain maintaining its evolutionary dominance over the empathic brain attempting to emerge.

Selfish ego becomes the fearful amygdala's protagonist, its defender against a world of perceived threats. In Freud's perfectly apt words, ego is the **"face turned toward reality,"** that is, the amygdala's reality. And so, the selfish ego is a neural network of collaboration between a biochemically fearful amygdala, a hippocampus storing indoctrinated and learned fear memories, and a subservient frontal cortex strategizing for socioeconomic superiority within a community perceived not with the feelings of kinship, but with an apprehension for threatening competitors; pursuing not common interest, but private interest; loyal not to democratic equality, but personal superiority—upper-class advantages not amenable to democratic principles or procedures. All unrestrained due to the absence of right brain moral sensibility.

Birth has been a "choice" between three fundamental human beings: fear induced selfishness, which is life negating; the less fear-based, more sanguine and confident and trusting personality, which is life affirming; and the brain of debilitating fear-based anxiety, free from amygdala instilled selfishness, but struggling to find confidence and identity and a place to be free from its psychological oppressions. The hyper-amygdala brain will spend a lifetime building forts; the empathic brain a lifetime despairing of a fortified world; and the anxious brain simply trying to find a path to tranquility.

. . . .

Genetics and emotional response to experience form the early brain through the reinforcement and pruning of neurons and synapses; they build the fences that define and limit who we can be. That is, the neurons that remain, and the circuits they form, will determine the mind we have. If we are ever to be truly free and somewhat self-reclaimed, the prefrontal cortex must jump that fence, to criticize our past formations and choose the experiences (cognitive and behavior modification practices) that will serve to expand our present selves into an exploration for what we might have been—and still can be. Full self-realization means forever looking in the mirror and seeing the self not yet reflected.

"...every psychoanalyst has seen patients who have been able to reverse the trends which seemed to determine

their lives, once they become aware of them and make a concentrated effort to regain their freedom." (Erich Fromm; *The Heart of Man,* 1964).

We can do this by seeing our conscious self as distinct from our brain machine... that our brain has thought and behavior patterns incurred through years of conditioning that we did not choose, but that we—the conscious self—can choose to alter through new thoughts and experiences and altered behaviors, repeated until the brain reconditions—neuroplasticity—to our more chosen self. We can do this through self-determination, supported by knowing it can be done.

The making of a human life involves many alternative characteristics—eye color, hand preference, gender—but the most profound distinction is the presence or absence of the capacity for empathy, whether one emerges at the threshold of life as a humanitarian or a sociopath. The distinction between caring and not caring for others of one's species is a measure of brain difference that would be easy to consider a distinction in kind—an evolutionary split of Homo sapiens into Homo empathicus and Homo egoisticus.

Indeed, Homo egoisticus is lagging in his biological adaptation, lingering in the neurology of amygdala fear, kept in his primal past by conformance to a competitive economic ideology... and his resistance to an economics of common security, where incentive does not reward selfish individualism, but rather a humanitarian self-interest in the well-being of the whole community. In contrast, the Homo empathicus brain is progressive, eager to adapt in anticipation of the technological possibility for a security-based economics that relieves the human brain from fear and competitive conflict, whence evolution can proceed beyond survival to an exploration of possibility, facing the unfamiliar and the uncertain with curiosity and intelligence.

From the beginning the natural world has told us who we cannot be, by telling us who we must be—what traits we must hold onto, and which we must forsake in order to survive. We are creatures made by environment. But gradually man has learned to make his own micro environment, his social habitat. We have told ourselves we must be selfish and competitive to survive. And so, we insist on a social habitat that demands selfish competition. We constrain ourselves from possibility because of our spiritual and emotional timidity; we embrace beliefs that console our fears rather than knowledge that creates understanding and the courage for advancement.

We must come to believe that a creature subject to environmental determination can remake the environment to remake himself, to condition himself into a better angel. Maybe there will be time to do that if we don't tinker too much with the macro environment: We can't destroy Nature, but we can change her to the point where she will destroy us. Despite all our hubris and godly self-image, environment made us, and it will end us. It seems likely that eternal survival is not in the cards for any form of life. Somewhere in the deck a fatal microbe or monster asteroid is inevitable. But it would be nice if our demise is the tragic end of a grand creature, and not the mere erasure of an ignoble egoist who soiled the cradle of life.

Imagine a primeval encounter between two hunters, each of a different clan, discovering they stalk the same prey. They fall upon it simultaneously and achieve its death. One, with a less fearful amygdala proceeds to share, but when his back is turned the other, suspicious and fearful of the other's intent, and greedy for his own abundance, preempts the threat by clubbing the other to death, taking the prize for himself.

From the point of view of his clan the selfish hunter's act was productive. He was hard working; he was a successful provider—predatory selfishness paid off. Of course, the clan of the deceased, when they find him, recognizing that the dent in his head did not come from the jaws of a beast, would go tracking the other club wielder, which would not be difficult because he is dragging home a carcass, whereupon they would apply retribution. A moment in time with a chance for friendship and cooperation, but fear and greed chose enmity.

This little parable reveals the self-defeating short-sightedness of selfish ego—immediate gain often entails longer term penalties that far outweigh the initial reward. And it clearly reveals fear-based selfishness as the source of evil. It also portrays the prophetic warning that injustice does not go unpunished. And it displays the initial disadvantage of trust and goodness: evil strikes first. Whenever fairness and generosity have turned their back, selfish greed has sought triumph and dominion. Indeed, it is the trust of the unselfish that enhances the opportunities of the selfish; and the absence of regulation that invites the corrupt disposition.

(Think conservative dirty tricks and liberal naivete', which is explained by the presence or absence of right brain moral sensibility. That is, only a frontal cortex without a moral conscience is eager to become proficient at deviousness. The selfish brain plots for advantage because it is driven by fear-reaction strategies; the non-selfish brain is restrained by its sense of fairness because it is less driven by fear. One thing is certain, selfishness is not naive! It knows the tricks of winning and relishes using them—the pleasure of triumph. The fearful brain knows that deceit is an ally, that undiscovered lies are expedient, that misrepresentation often makes the sale. Also, we tend to understand others by what we know of ourselves. Thus, if we do not harbor duplicitous thoughts, we are often naive before those who do. The reverse is also true: the selfish brain is filled with cynicism about the good intentions of others—recall the conservative ridicule of "do-gooders". Selfishness is completely dismayed at altruism, and in that absence of mind lies the birthplace of evil. A democratic people must be mindful of the incentives they allow, for the behavior they reward is the behavior they will get).

There is a mental condition known as "Amusia." It is an inability to process musical sounds into a joyful experience... to feel an inner synchronicity with rhythm and melody. It is a functional "deafness" of the brain, equivalent to the blindness of an undeveloped visual cortex. Amusia serves as an analogy for the lack of empathic sensibility, the inability to experience sympathy for others.

Similarly, we all have known people without a sense of humor, or who lack an ability for inspirational responses to art, or the wonders of nature. Of course, we would not want a person who suffers from amusia conducting an orchestra. Do we want the functionally unempathic brain conducting our democratic community?! Do we want those absent an empathic faculty representing others in government when they do not care about others? In fact, recent research has associated high empathy and musical appreciation with human social interaction.

Empathy is the last thing the conservative mind wants in government. Such a mind does not want government making equal those over whom it wishes to be superior. Hence, the conservative opposition to a government that would **"secure these rights"** through social programs. The opposition to taxation is not only the complaint of greed, it is also a political strategy for financially incapacitating government from its democratic purpose of promoting the general welfare.

The lack of empathic feeling is an inability to hear the music, the orchestra, of the common good; ears that do not hear the music, hearts that cannot join the dance.

"Though seeing, they do not see; though hearing, they do not hear or understand...For this people's heart has become calloused." (Matthew 13:13-16).

It was once believed that women, and men without property were not competent to vote. Maybe fear constructed brains are not competent to vote. Maybe voter qualification should depend on brain scans. Maybe if you do not care about others because you neurologically cannot care about others you should not be legislating and administering socioeconomic policy. It is said the beginning of wisdom lies in knowing thyself. That seems truer than ever—along with knowing who the other is!

CHAPTER TWO

THOUGHTS ON CLASSICAL LIBERALISM

The justification of private property in classical liberal thought is most clearly expressed in John Locke's *Two Treatises on Government* (published anonymously in 1689).

Locke argued that what a man removed from the common provisions of nature through personal labor, in gathering those things necessary for his preservation, became his private property—as long as there was **"enough, and as good left in common for others."** (John Locke, Book 2; chap. 5).

The amount of property was limited by the notion of spoilage: if what was taken from the commons spoiled before being used then too much was appropriated. Locke later circumvented his notion of limitation by reference to money, a commodity that could be accumulated without spoilage.

It was inferred from Locke's text that the advent of money, a mode of exchange accepted by everyone, and which allowed for storage of extensive property without spoilage, implied consent and justification to accumulation and inequality. This is merely assertion, not reasoning—the common acceptance of money as a convenient device for exchanging goods and services does not justify its unlimited accumulation... *can* does not imply *ought*; and it certainly does not imply a universal consent to inequality. Convenience is not a principle. In fact, Locke's own assertion denies the inference:

"...no Man could ever have a just power over another by Right of property in land or Possessions." (Two Treatises, Book 1, chap. 4).

Unlimited accumulation of property is what gives **"power over another."** Inequality is not justified because money is not subject to spoilage.

The Natural Law limit on property is not spoilage, but exclusion of others from their necessity, their entitlement to the material support of their lives and development—which Locke explicitly recognized by the qualifier **"enough, and as good left in common for others."** Money is simply a claim on goods: whoever possesses all the money has the power to possess all the goods. Locke sought a philosophic argument for the justification of private property to undermine the divine right of kings and land holding aristocrats. It was a laudable and democratic purpose. But arguments from natural law imply equality, not inequality. The class societies of Locke's time were not ready for equality (Is that why Two Treatises was published anonymously? And why Locke exiled to Holland?)

By allowing money to justify inequality of property, Locke abandoned his labor justification of property. For if the conditions of spoilage and enough left for others no longer applied then neither did the justification of ownership by labor. Serfs had labored for centuries. Those who most labored had always been furthest from ownership. And further, private possession through labor presupposes access to common land upon which to labor. As the commons were increasingly enclosed into private property—as in 18th century England—access to common land upon which to labor was increasingly limited. Removing the means to an end precludes the end.

Unequal property possession remained a fact without a legitimate origin (still does). While a basic property in the materials that fulfill and secure the right to life is clearly a natural right, an excess of those materials is not. *Government is instituted to secure natural rights*, not to secure a "freedom" to possess an extent of property that deprives others from their natural right to access the provisions of nature; or subordinates them to an inferior social position in exchange for granting them a minimum subsistence; an affront that would be avenged were there no government defending the affront.

Neither would Classical Liberalism accept a definition of property as based on an original common ownership, or common non-ownership—everyone's right to everything, or no one's right to anything. Either way that would imply equality. And property possession had historically been unequal. So, the property interest needed an argument for the origin of property that justified unequal possession. But it did not want a justification that implied a limitation on the extent of ownership, nor a right of the deprived to appropriation based on need. If there was to be a justification of unlimited private property it would have to explain property's origin and its unequal possession in terms of rights rather than mere historical fact.

Neither would Adam Smith's *The Wealth of Nations* provide that justification; his argument simply begins with property already having been appropriated; the original "right" of ownership presumably determined by the power to possess and defend, with no obligation upon the appropriator and no provision to the dispossessed. Where in nature the excesses of selfishness are exposed to retribution, in classical liberal society the excessive possessions of selfishness would be protected by law—government is not instituted to secure equal rights; government is for protecting and facilitating the traditions of inequality. However, Smith also seemed to waver by acknowledging that:

"...civil government, so far as it is instituted for the security of property, is in reality instituted for the defense of the rich against the poor, or of those who have some property against those who have none at all." (Adam Smith; *Wealth of Nations*; bk. 5, ch.1)

The Declaration of Independence did not mention property as an unalienable right:

"...the Jefferson party formed upon the supposed superior devotion to the personal rights of men, holding the rights of property to be secondary only and greatly inferior." (Abraham Lincoln; *Letter*, April 6, 1859).

Adam Smith had stated the first premise of Classical Liberalism in one sentence:

"Every man, as long as he does not violate the laws of justice, is left perfectly free to pursue his own interest his own way." (*Wealth of Nations*, bk.4, ch.9).

This remains the basic principle of Classical Liberalism, "Neoliberalism" being the modern label. And the conditional phrase about violation of the laws of justice continues to be the unavoidable caveat; that is, *freedom is subject to the requirements of justice*. The political argument is about what the laws of justice require; that is, where the balance between every man's freedom to achieve his interest and every one's protection (liberty) from the consequences of those interests should lie. The questions are: how much regulation of individual freedom, and what social outcomes are acceptable in a democratic community founded on the principle of human equality? The duty of democratic government is to protect and secure the natural rights of individuals against the interest of others to subordinate them.

The term "liberal" has undergone a transformation in its roughly 240 years journey. Generally, liberal refers to the political freedom of the individual from arbitrary authority. Political liberalism had turned absolute monarchy into constitutional monarchy through the introduction of a parliament. Classical liberalism and neoliberalism are about the *economic* freedom of the individual from government regulation and redistribution of any unequal outcome. The result of economic freedom was a new path to political and social inequality based on wealth inequality. So, liberalism broke into factions which continue today: the free-market, small government liberals, are the anti-regulation, anti-tax Libertarians and conservative Republicans. Those who believe in regulation of economic activity and adjustment of outcomes for a more fair and equal society are liberal Democrats. The emergence of neoliberalism in the era of Thatcher and Reagan was a reaction against New Deal government intervention in the economy for greater social justice and security. The political success of neoliberalism under Reagan, in winning over the working class, was based on cultural issues—race and abortion—not economic policy. The Democrats were intimidated, and unnecessarily conceded on economic policy; baited by the Republicans into fighting cultural issues, rightfully defending the victims of racism and bigotry. But they lost the white working class and turned into economic neoliberals. The Democrats, in losing the working class, turned to the upper class… and rule by money.

But all of this being said, American democracy remains in the hands of the common people. If the majority is consigned to economic and social inequality it is done by their own neglect. Contributing to the neglect is the fact that people come to identify with political labels and popularized personalities instead of thoroughly understanding their interests and the broader issues that impact them; a consequence of illiberal indoctrination and poor education.

. . . .

The most prominent proposal for the economic freedom of selfishness was Adam Smith's 18th century inquiry into *The Wealth of Nations*. Smith argued that the greatest economic wealth would result if individuals were free to pursue their natural self-interest without interference from the state. The argument gave impetus to the demand for the freedom of common people from centuries of social and economic domination by kings and priests and hereditary aristocracies. As with Locke's argument for private property, *The Wealth of Nations* was a great advance in the process of liberalization. But in the new freedom an old impulse, the selfish brain—Christianity's original sin—would find a new path to social domination.

Smith begins with a description of the productive powers of labor and **"the order, according to which its produce is naturally distributed among the different ranks"** of society. Smith goes on:

"This original state of things, in which the labourer (sic) enjoyed the whole produce of his own labour, could not last beyond the first introduction of the appropriation of land...it would be to no purpose to trace further what might have been..." (Book 1, ch 8).

This was an extraordinary concession to existing conditions (an unavoidable reality of the times if one wished to survive), and some would think a reprehensible avoidance of judgment. Adam Smith was not inquiring about a system of economic organization based on a fair and just distribution of resources among naturally equal human beings. He begins with an acceptance of land already privately **"appropriated,"** and a society divided into **"ranks."** His **"natural"** distribution of wealth assumed existing inequality. As for the justice of land appropriation and the proper distribution of wealth among social ranks, or even the rightness of ranks, Smith evades:

"I shall not take upon me to determine." (ibid. Book 1, ch 8).

Classical Liberalism thus begins with an acceptance of the existing social divisions and the unequal possession of property. Mankind's historical campaign for freedom and liberty was against existing inequalities, not a search for an alternative method of imposing and maintaining them. And so, the capitalist ideology is not very concerned for the rights of life, nor the implications for equality and material security. We can see that the ideology of selfishness uses insecurity as incentive, and is more desirous of the opportunity for selfish ambitions to achieve inequality than providing for the general welfare.

The Wealth of Nations was published in 1776, an interesting historical coincidence with the American Declaration of Independence... the founding of the nation destined to realize the potential of Adam Smith's argument for unbridled economic self-interest more than any other. Smith's book was the seminal work of a new order of society which was beginning to emerge from the long centuries of serfdom and land-owning lords.

Individual artisans were separating themselves from the landed estates and collecting in the growing towns and cities to sell the products of their labor. They were the early practitioners of the "entrepreneurial spirit" in the expanding age of commerce. *The Wealth of Nations* rationalized this struggle for economic independence—the desire of common individuals to raise themselves out of the poverty and servitude of serfdom, and the rigid divisions of class society. The artisans and traders who did well began to accumulate an excess of revenue beyond the needs of their own subsistence—the creation of capital.

(It would later be argued by Laissez-faire—**"let things alone"**—economists that it is the economic independence of private wealth and property that guarantees political freedom; hence the supposed necessary link between capitalism and democracy. Of course, it would not guarantee the political freedom of those who lost in the competition for wealth and property, and all those who were not propertied white men. It is argued here that the link is specious, that capitalism is opposed to democratic equality; that unregulated capitalism inevitably results in inequalities that violate democratic forms and principles).

Adam Smith's argument was that the greatest aggregate material wealth would be produced if individuals were left free to pursue their own economic interest. And he further argued that although private interest would undoubtedly be motivated by selfish intentions, the unseen logic of the process—the **"invisible hand"** and the principle of **"unintended consequences"**—would result in a beneficial outcome to the community as a whole; that selfishness, despite its intentions, would be guided to a socially desirable outcome. The implicit—and noticeably not explicit—assurance was that the increase of wealth would be equitably distributed—the modern version being "trickle down". And, in addition, as each person knew best their own desires, freedom from regulation was necessary to maximize happiness. Of course, there is no basis for assuming that unintended consequences will be good more often than bad, especially when it is selfishness that is encouraged and rewarded. And as for the freedom of desires to maximize happiness, that is what necessitates laws that regulate social behavior. *There is no right to a pursuit of happiness that does harm to the life and rights of others.*

Similar to the invisible hand, F.A. Hayek (*The Constitution of Liberty*) argued that when individuals are free from government regulation, they will produce a natural, or **"spontaneous order"** that is more economically efficient and productive than would be a system designed by government; that "central planners" cannot know all that is necessary to know. The objection picks on a non-issue: a democratic government's regulation is not about planning and designing what and how much to produce, but rectifying democratically unacceptable outcomes.

"Spontaneous order" is an argument for efficiency and productivity that is value neutral. There is no judgment of outcomes, and only a materialistic vision of a good society. *Efficiency can be productive of evil as well as good.* Without rules, spontaneity might even produce chaos and ruinous conflict rather than a good and beneficial order. And it certainly will produce an "order" that represents the preferences of the most influential—the desires of the prevailing powers. The spontaneous order of Good and Evil is humanity's enduring and unfortunate dilemma.

The classical liberal and neoliberal passion for the freedom of selfishness was, however, a value judgment—it valued private economic freedom over the purpose of democratic government to secure the equal rights of life for all... it promoted an individual right to achieve superiority over democracy's promise of equality. It is selfishness making an anti-democracy argument for its freedom. A spontaneous order that results from unregulated selfish ambitions is very likely to be much less fair and equal than an order that would result from rules and regulations—and tax policies—that prevent undemocratic consequences.

Efficiently producing social inequality is not a democratic outcome.

And that is what we are arguing: the selfish brain is not democratic; it is an authoritarian personality with aristocratic pretensions. Selfishness abhors governments that regulate. Regulating the sociopath and empowering the humanitarian would make a much better spontaneous order. In fact, Hayek had no idea where spontaneous order would arrive, he is making an argument for a freedom that excludes considerations of morality and justice:

"...the liberal (Hayek means economic liberal, not political liberal) **position is based on...a preparedness to let change run its course even if we cannot predict where it will lead."** (*Why I Am Not a Conservative*) (Parenthesis added).

The economic question is not capitalism or socialism—whether a minority of private citizens, or a minority of party members control economic resources and extract upper-class privileges. The important question is: what economic forms of production and distribution fulfill the promise of democracy—that **"all men are created equal."** Free markets go a long way to fulfilling democracy's promise, until the unequal transference of economic wealth to private ownership begins to corrupt democracy—becomes private interest and power eclipsing the public good. As with any expression of freedom, laws and regulations are required to make it beneficial and not harmful to democratic principles. Laissez-faire capitalism gives permission to all intentions and approval to all outcomes... and is more compatible with authoritarian political forms than with a popular sovereignty that might awaken to its rights.

Classical liberalism relied on an aggressive human behavior, what Smith called the **"selfish propensity"** of individuals to acquire greater and greater amounts of wealth. And it required a large number of hungry laborers—serfs forced from land-based subsistence by changes in land laws:

"...the natural effort of every individual to better his own condition, when suffered to exert itself with freedom and security." (*The Wealth of Nations*; bk.4, ch.5)

Smith's phrase, **"suffered to exert itself"** is key to understanding a system of competition for survival. It means intended insecurity (conservative opposition to "safety nets" and union organizers). That is, it would not be government's role to secure the right to life, but to give freedom to a fear driven instinct for self-preservation, and political protection—property rights—to the consequences: **"with freedom and security."** Every man's insecurity would give the most aggressively ambitious an opportunity to gain advantage, and to then extort further advantage. Peasants forced off land subsistence would be cheap labor for the factories (Anti-unionism and racism and religious divisions and class privilege would later serve to keep the peasants unorganized, uneducated and divided, thus powerless).

A democratic government, **"instituted to secure these rights,"** would form institutions that protect the human brain from the stresses and derangements of fear and perpetual insecurity, and protect human rights (liberty) from the predatory freedoms of greed. The selfish mind wants democratic political authority ceded to market interests, economic power controlling political power in order to forestall the slow advance of democratic equality. Greed wants advantage, not equality. *It is the sociopath who ascends because there is no morally inspired hesitancy to his ambitions.* Classical liberalism sought to confine the lower orders of humanity to the unending anxieties of an economic system founded on the usefulness of human insecurity to the ambitions of sociopaths.

Systematically denying social security in order to exert and control insecure people is not a system of freedom. It is systemic coercion. Classical liberalism's love of **"opportunity"** means an opportunity to gain the assets that give control of society.

Classical liberal "freedom" is that of a prisoner allowed to run for his life, who is never caught and never escapes, but must never stop running. That is not freedom, it is a cruel promise manipulating the dream of freedom.

"It is not...difficult to foresee which of the two parties must...have the advantage...and force the other into a compliance with their terms." (*The Wealth of Nations*, bk.1, ch.8)

In one sentence Adam Smith acknowledges the true **"invisible hand"** of Classical Liberalism—the coercion behind the free and voluntary veneer. What begins in theory as voluntary associations and exchanges matures in practice to involuntary submission to socioeconomic hierarchy. The democratic promise of freedom and equality submits to the exigencies and consequences of economic competition... the "free market" creates a financial aristocracy.

"The most specious thing to be said, is, that he that is Proprietor of the whole world, may deny all the rest of Mankind Food, and so at his pleasure starve them, if they will not acknowledge his Sovereignty, and obey his will... And therefore, no Man could ever have a just Power over the Life of another by Right of property in Land or Possessions... a Man can no more justly make use of another's necessity... than he that has more strength can seize upon a weaker, master him to his Obedience, and with a Dagger at his throat offer him Death or Slavery." (John Locke; *Two Treatises of Government*; Book 1, chap 41).

The quote from Locke is the classic statement for the precedence of human rights over property rights. Which also means the good of a democratic community over the freedom of avarice to achieve unjust advantages. Adam Smith's "invisible hand" assurances had obscured the risk of social injustice, and other yet to be perceived evils in the systematic encouragement of selfishness. And his faith in "unintended consequences" simply assumed that conscious self-seeking would result in some derivative good to others—that some good "trickles down" from a selfish dynamic. That it also results in trickle down wrongs to others he only cautioned:

"The proposal of any new law or regulation of commerce which comes from this order (the business interest) **ought always to be listened to with great precaution... It comes from an order of men whose interest is never exactly the same with that of the public, who have generally an interest to deceive and even to oppress the public, and who accordingly, have upon many occasions, both**

deceived and oppressed it." (*The Wealth of Nations*, bk.1, ch.11) (Parenthesis added).

Why not, then, put up guardrails against this order of men? Why play a game of chance between justice and injustice... between good and evil? Why not systematically require justice instead of conceding opportunity to injustice? Adam Smith knew he was freeing the reptile, and that he was relying on the reptile's intentions being thwarted by an unintended fate. It was a philosophic gamble that selfish ambitions would not achieve their intended consequences. As it turned out the gamble was a loss--the invisible hand was a sleight of hand, an illusory assurance that failed to prevent the inevitable outcome—the reality of wealth inequality. But as a deception it worked. The reptile got his freedom; the common man believed the assurance... as usual.

"...the wondering cheated multitude worshiped the invention." (Thomas Paine; ibid.).

Was Adam Smith a philosopher whose mystical logic failed, or a propagandist who succeeded? Whichever, by invoking the invisible hand as an assurance of good to the community, Smith was acknowledging the risk of selfish interest to the common good. *For if the freedom of selfishness was a good thing why must its promised beneficence be unintended*? Why not reward those who intend beneficence... and skip the moral gamble and mystical postulates?

Smith was claiming that the unregulated economic actions of individuals will result in an outcome that is wise and good, efficient and productive. But what logic guarantees that a multitude of "free" individual actions will be wise and good, or even arrive at a best outcome, *or that a better outcome would not result from a restriction on bad actions.* The visible logic of unregulated free markets is inevitable inequality (and pervasive corruption), as initial advantages are leveraged into greater advantages; and less advantage accelerates downwards into less and less opportunity and poorer life prospects. As for efficient and productive, for what product? As inequality increases wealth attracts resources to less necessary luxury productions and away from more basic social goods like education and healthcare and public works... and food to eat. Pandering to "elite" self-indulgence has little social value. *Efficiently produced mega yachts matter less than properly paid teachers and affordable healthcare.*

What satisfies the requirements of justice in a democratic community is distributed wealth, not aggregate wealth. "Unintended consequences" was a ruse in the guise of an assurance that the distribution would be fair. With the hindsight of nearly two and a half centuries it is clear that the actual consequence of exerted selfishness is great social inequality and insecurity (not to mention the reinforcement of the amygdala's fear), and it is very much intended. Sometimes consequences are unjust, but slow to be apprehended. Such has been the legacy of the freedom of selfishness: competition between id dominated egos has alienated individuals away from human sociability; "suffered to exert themselves" against others in a struggle to survive that has led to isolation and loneliness, and the ongoing natural selection of the avaricious brain.

An important distinction needs to be made regarding "selfish propensity." All life forms share a natural self-interest in survival. But natural self-interest only justifies one's equality, the desire not to be disadvantaged, not to be deprived of life, and one's share of the materials and conditions of survival. It does not justify the desire to extract from others, or to hoard the provisions of nature, nor the presumption of personal superiority. Rational self-interest does not require unlimited reward. "Selfish propensity" as applied to unregulated capitalism is the psychological disposition to escape one's insecurity by appropriating more than one's share; in effect, taking from others——in the context of this hypothesis it is a fear dominated brain uninformed by the moral concepts of common interest and cooperative achievement; and emotionally unequipped for compassion for others. The absence of empathy (sociopathy) has been throughout the whole course of human history the root and core of crime and social conflict. It is those who fear so much for themselves and care so little for others who have sought to become the possessors of power and privilege and extreme abundance—whatever the butchery required. Classical liberalism gave what had historically been overt conquest and oppression by force an economic path to legitimacy... justified as freedom of the individual. Natural self-interest entails the right of self-defense and an expectation of social equality. Classical Liberalism exaggerated that self-interest into a compulsive selfishness, driven by insecurity, fracturing community and making the rights of life a reward of competitive success.

If human nature is seen as having evolved by a long and painful crawl out of the depths of primordial fear, then to accept man's condition at any historical stopping place as his nature, and design societal arrangements which exert and reinforce that nature, is to confine him to that historical moment, precluding the possibilities of his further evolution. Whatever one chooses to call that, it is not respecting freedom.

The exertion of man's insecurity in order to compel his efforts has been productive of material prosperity for much of mankind—when masters prosper slaves have a chance to eat better. But the persistence of insecurity has moored human character to its primitive past. What manner of human character would emerge were fear no longer the primary motivator of behavior may one day be known. But for us, still immersed in selfish pursuits, unregulated capitalism is a restraint, not a step in the direction of a promising human evolution.

Adaptability is supposed essential to survival, the inhabitant must change if the habitat requires it. It would seem an ideology that concedes to the *emotions* of fear rather than relieving the *conditions* of fear, is not the best strategy for advancement. And acknowledging capitalism's productivity does not mean there was, or is no alternative. It is not individual selfishness that is productive, but intelligence and imagination and aspiration, and a simple work ethic. The Enlightenment's release of human reason from religious superstition and persecution released the human mind to thoughts of science and technology... and freedom. Homo Empathicus has no less desire for material progress than Homo Egoisticus. It is a matter of what human character is encouraged by rewarding incentives, and what intentions control the capital that supports enterprise.

Much argument in support of traditional arrangements relies on the notion of "tacit consent," i.e., acceptance with silent complaint. In reality, unjust circumstances begin with imposition, followed by no-recourse resignation, to then fossilize into traditions transmitted through indoctrination. That a circumstance has not been opposed by a predecessor does not establish its rightness. Justice is a current voice, whether or not spoken or heard in the past. And even where a prior consent existed, it is not prescriptive in the present. The natural rights of the individual life are paramount, and how a democratic people evolve into a new understanding of their rights supersedes prior understandings. What our predecessors decided or accepted for themselves has less weight than what we desire and decide for ourselves. That a tradition is long-standing does not imply rightness in the present, nor even rightness in its beginning, only that the people it favored had the power to impose it. The silence of the disadvantaged never implies acceptance, only a submission that is the fate of the powerless.

Adam Smith could argue that government was not for:

"...superintending the industry of private people, and of directing it towards the employments most suitable to the interests of the society." (*The Wealth of Nations*).

Yet he could also assert:

"...those exertions of the natural liberty of a few individuals, which might endanger the security of the whole society, are, and ought to be, restrained by the laws of all governments." (ibid).

In reading Adam Smith, it seems that every theoretical proposal is qualified by a following practical caution. Thus, selfishness both serves and disserves the public good; government should both restrain and not restrain the selfish propensity. There is no reconciling the contradictions, only an assertion that emphasizes the recommendation while distracting from the caution—that selfish propensity will be beneficial to the whole of society. Smith's argument is, in effect, that selfishness is a bad thing but its avarice will produce economic wealth, and despite its hoarding intention it will result in beneficial good to the community, however unintended ("trickle down"). The risk to the community, however, is that the intention to private power over the community would be achieved; *such is the oligarchic world we live in.* Of course, the free-market ideologues run full speed with Smith's freedom of selfishness and ignore his reservations—because his reservations reveal their not-so-secret intentions. It is up to an enlightened democratic sensibility to impose the regulations of selfish individualism that would honor Adam Smith's reservations.

Edmond Burke:

"Men qualify for civil liberty in exact proportion to their disposition to put moral chains upon their own appetites; in proportion as their love of justice is above their rapacity... Society cannot exist unless a controlling power upon the will and appetite be placed somewhere, and the less of it there is within, the more there must be without...men of intemperate minds cannot be free. Their passions forge their fetters." (Letter to a Member of the French Assembly; January 19, 1791).

It must be stated that one cannot know Adam Smith and *The Wealth of Nations*, without also knowing his *Theory of Moral Sentiments*, which Smith considered his major work. The latter contains many observations difficult to reconcile with an advocacy for a culture of competitive selfishness. A greater exposition of this point would be too much for this already lengthy argument. I will offer a few quotations, and leave it at that:

"...that to feel much for others and little for ourselves, that to restrain our selfish, and to indulge our benevolent affections, constitutes the perfection of human nature." (Adam Smith; *Theory of Moral Sentiments*, 1:1:5).

"...how disagreeable does he appear to be, whose hard and obdurate heart feels for himself only, but is altogether insensible to the happiness or misery of others." (ibid; 1:1:5).

"...that composure and tranquility of mind which is so necessary to happiness, and which is best promoted by the... passions of gratitude and love." (ibid; 1:2:3).

"Society may subsist, though not in the most comfortable state, without beneficence; but the prevalence of injustice must utterly destroy it." (ibid; 2:2:3).

"To the intention or affection of the heart... all approbation or disapprobation must ultimately belong." (Ibid; 2:3: intro).

And so, *The Wealth of Nations*, published at the time of the great Declaration of democratic equality, did not anticipate or recommend that equality. Social competition for individual and class advantage in a context of scarcity of the basic materials of well-being will someday, if mankind survives the amygdala's fear, become an anachronism. Yet, for Smith's time, competition for wealth was consistent with the historical reality of class inequality and the acceptance of unrepentant selfishness as the nature of man. Economics will continue to determine politics until the social injustice perpetuated by unregulated selfishness is no longer tolerated. It will then become time for the politics of justice to determine the economics of democratic equality; time for everyone to realize that *great inequality of economic wealth is a violation of the American Declaration for equal and inalienable rights.* As fear is our maker, a modicum of selfishness is understandable, and indeed inevitable, yet manageable so long as its reward is not great.

It is tempting to wonder if the true Adam Smith was revealed in the *Theory of Moral Sentiments* (1759), while the Smith of selfish propensity (1776), some 17 years later, was the result of personal evolution, or enlistment as an intellectual mercenary in the pay of Classical Liberalism—a harbinger of the modern think tanker? Maybe the younger Smith was the idealist, less advanced in the world—youth untainted by expedience—and the older Smith more associated with, and accommodated by, status quo interests? (*It would be fascinating to hear if he would think today that his invisible hand has served his moral sentiments*). It would have been so easy to have advocated a certain freedom and reasonable incentive to the innovative and productive energies of a fair-minded self-interest, while at the same time proposing just restraints upon the ambitions of avarice, rather than risk the likelihood of its much intended consequences. Adam Smith preached moral sentiments, but he rewarded selfish propensity; he promised materialistic benefits, but sacrificed human character. He knew that men were not angels, but he concealed the moral reality with a mystical belief that avarice would aim at selfish ends and hit the common good. Within himself, Adam Smith represents the drama of human hypocrisy: the pursuit of personal wealth and its attendant power, accompanied by flirtations with moral sentiments; praising the angel above while feeding the reptile within. The amygdala brain has discarded the sentiments—though not the pretension, and so easily avoids, in its own mind, the conscious violations of conscience, and the embarrassments of hypocrisy.

(Adam Smith preceded Charles Darwin. Perhaps if they could have had a conversation, Smith would have understood he was engaging in social selection, and bestowing a continuation of the reptilian brain upon the future).

Smith's uncritical assumption of some original unequal appropriation about which he found no purpose **"in tracing further,"** and no desire for himself to **"determine the rightness of,"** resulted in the justification and reinforcement of human selfishness, and acceptance (approval?) of the unjust origins of property-based inequality. If Adam Smith could have found a rightful historical beginning to the unequal appropriation of Nature's provisions, he would have surely announced it... his patrons would have been so eternally grateful.

The philosophers and academics of previous times were in need of patrons. Academic freedom and tenured professorships are modern quasi-protections for the freedom of thought that did not exist in those earlier times. All works in the history of ideas must be read with an eye on the historical context: what the author dare not say, on the one side; and what he must say, on the other. Philosophy had to please its patronage. And often when it did not the philosopher suffered the consequence; self-preservation recommended not antagonizing those to whom one was vulnerable—still does. The political and religious persecution—and crucifixion—of truth seekers and justice seekers is the modus operandi of the desire for dominance. Even today there is political reticence among scientists and academics—peer standing and academic reputation and research grants are effective inhibitors of intellectual risk-taking. Calling things what they are and standing for what one believes to be true and right, over what is personally safe or politically expedient or job securing, is the essence of intellectual independence and personal honor, but not always easy to display—an example of how economic dependency compromises the freedom of character and conscience. And beyond the shadow of threat waits the hemlock… *Principled opposition to powerful interests is not a commonplace courage.*

Can a democratic people find the determination to make *a new dedication to the principles of democracy*, and build new institutions that reward a better view of human nature? If one begins by removing Smith's assumption of land already privately appropriated, and his acceptance of social ranks, and instead begins with The Declaration's assertion of **"created equal"** and **"unalienable rights,"** a whole new economic regime would emerge. Natural self-interest would be respected, self-sufficiency and innovation would be honored, reasonable profit would accrue to merit, while sociopathic selfishness would no longer be encouraged or respected. The great fear of privileged elites is that the commoners will rediscover their natural rights and reclaim their liberty.

The essential notions that underlie our forms of inequality are: that selfish ego is natural and therefore its freedom justified; that private property is a freedom not subject to limitation by natural, or civil, law; that economic productivity requires human selfishness. All three notions are false in fact, and are but ideological premises, precepts postulated to justify The Ideology of Selfishness. The real end of history will arrive when laissez-faire capitalism is fully regulated by democratic rather than individualist purposes; *a democratic capitalism rather than a capitalist democracy.* Then will be the beginning of a new history when the human brain will escape the formations of fear, no longer constrained and conditioned to social conflict, whereupon a true individualism will find a true freedom in the security given by a common and equal liberty and justice for all.

The special talent of selfishness is to make enemies where there might otherwise be friends. The future of humanity will need more friends.

Twenty-four centuries ago, Plato had argued that private property encouraged greed and social conflict. Classical liberalism welcomed the greed, and honored it with "freedom"... And sent the serfs to wage the conflict!

A democratic people must recognize that there is no means so pure that it justifies any outcome; that there is no right to a freedom, or right of property, that justifies the superiority of a few and the inferiority of many. All the classical liberals and neoliberals and libertarians tell us the freedom of the individual to achieve his personal desires is the highest good, and thus wherever his freedom takes us must also be good—"spontaneous order"... the means justifies the end. This has been the successful sophistry of economic liberalism since Adam Smith only because it favors the existing elites and establishments who largely control the propagation of ideas—and tell the lies that misinform. A means is judged by the outcome it produces. When a different outcome is demanded it requires an altered means to produce it. By the way, "personal desire" does not justify unregulated freedom. If it did what would we do about serial killers?

The democratic principles that uphold the rights of Life and Liberty are our inheritance, defended and passed to us by prior sacrifices. Nothing outside of ourselves compels obedience and loyalty to the past, only when our sense of honor demands it from within; whereupon we embrace obligation and duty not because it profits us personally, but because it is payment for our debts to past sacrifice. Every generation chooses its place in history by what it stands for... and what it stands against.

CHAPTER THREE

BEYOND THE REPTILIAN BRAIN

"The fault, dear Brutus, is not in our stars, But in ourselves..." (*Julius Caesar*; 1, ii, 140-141).

By now anyone reading this text may—or may not—have wondered to themselves where they fall on the scale between ego and heart: Am I an egocentric conservative, conformed to fear-driven beliefs and prejudices and selfish ambitions, and resisting change that would relieve the hardships of others? Or am I heart, upholding principles of Right and Good, and struggling to live a compassionate and conscientious life, my inner self compromised by the selfish and materialistic values that success in the surrounding culture so widely demands? Or am I mired somewhere in between, short of both egoistic satisfactions and heart fulfillment?

Most of us, I suspect, find ourselves somewhere in the middle, struggling for security and hoping for at least some modest abundance, yet knowing our hearts are longing for a liberty that would give us the freedom to express our better selves; a liberty from material insecurity and the compassion-killing competition for "success". I believe it is extremely important for our human future that the great democratic majority choose heart—that they stand up for the liberty of their inner selves from the insecurity-based striving demanded by the Ideology of Selfishness; a liberty promised by the historical advance of democratic principles, and offered by the innovative and productive technologies of modern science. This will require that the public mind end its deference to the upper-class presumptions of elitism, and recognize that the optimum condition for a peaceful human evolution is mutual security, not "freedom" for fear-driven ambitions. *Good struggles in this world because Evil is so free.*

During the last awakening of democratic populism, spurred by the desperation of the Great Depression, Franklin Roosevelt offered these words in his State of the Union of 1935:

"We find our population suffering from old inequalities, little changed by past sporadic remedies. In spite of our efforts and in spite of our talk we have not weeded out the over privileged and we have not effectively lifted up the under privileged. Both of these manifestations of injustice have retarded happiness. No wise man has any intention of destroying what is known as the 'profit motive,' because by the profit motive we mean the right by work to earn a decent livelihood for ourselves and our families...
We have, however, a clear mandate from the people, that Americans must forswear that conception of the acquisition of wealth which, through excessive profits, creates undue private power over...public affairs. In building toward this end we do not destroy ambition... We continue to recognize the greater ability of some to earn more than others. But we do assert that the ambition of the individual to obtain for him and his, a proper security, a reasonable leisure, and a decent living throughout life is an ambition to be preferred to the

appetite for great wealth and great power...I place the security of the men, women, and children of the Nation first."

In the wake of the multi-decade conservative attack upon social liberal sensibilities it is time for the security of men, women and children to finally be placed first. I have no doubt that a poll of the American people would show overwhelming support for President Roosevelt's statement: that the security of ordinary people is more important to the Nation than the ambition of the selfish ego for private wealth and power. The problem is, private wealth and power control the political and economic instruments for making law and policy—and the propagandic talent to turn so many people against imagined enemies, and away from their personal interests. Until aggressive selfishness is checked by an aggressive and unselfish democratic majority with a view of their common liberties, the promise of democracy will remain words on a highly revered but little adhered to parchment. But can a revolution of awareness ever happen when **"the wondering cheated multitude"** select their rulers by the prominence of their celebrity rather than the truth of their ideas—when name recognition supersedes character? Can the **"cheated multitude"** save democracy?

"If we are to have another contest in the near future of our national existence, I predict that the dividing line will not be Mason's and Dixon's, but between patriotism and intelligence on one side, & superstition, ambition, & ignorance on the other." (President U.S. Grant, 1876).

The sea anchor that holds our course to the interests of the money elite is the ignorance and timidity that cannot see through the storms of fear, and the habits of compliance to the way things are. There is no inevitability to injustice. Only justice must be desired and demanded. But we are a materialistic culture, a people conditioned to a preference for immediate satisfaction, uninformed of the past, and insufficiently thoughtful of the future. The Nation's material success is also our illness—a satiated mind is no longer an inquiring mind, no longer fit for the discipline of learning, nor open to the wonderment that leads to discovery—of the outer world and one's inner self. Such a mind only seeks continuing amusements and ever more entertainments. It does not thrill to the motto: "duty, honor, country." It thrills only to the prospect of gain, more amusements and greater excitements—stimulation of the brain's pleasure center... a determined desire for the emotions of pleasure to eclipse the emotions of fear.

How, then, does a whole people, burdened with systemic insecurity, seeking relief through "fun" and distraction, turn to considerations of Truth and human possibility to find the systemic remedies for their fears? History gives no answer, only the example of murdered prophets and unheeded prophesies.

. . . .

To criticize the selfish ideology that rules America is not to criticize America. America began as a declaration that common people could rule themselves through a common allegiance to democratic rights and liberties, free of aristocratic elites, and free of authoritarian dictates. America is the sea to which all the dreams of freedom and liberty flow; including all the forsaken dreams that fell on the battlefield of history's past oppressions—the dreams of freedom not for selfish ego to gain dominion, but for the liberty of heart from unjust domination. Yet the culture of America succumbed to a selfish ideology that defies human equality. We had come from the old world with fears that were too deep; we saw opportunities that were too great; and felt compunctions that were too faint. And so, we enslaved Africans, exiled the Native Americans we did not murder from the lands we coveted, and conspired foreign wars to gain additional lands. We then killed each other in horrendous numbers over whether those black people would remain slaves; and when they were freed from legal slavery we watched as they were bonded again into a segregated and brutal inferiority—for another one hundred years! And across the land in California Native Americans were enslaved... and some exterminated for bounty. Our destiny was manifest: we would rob and murder our way to becoming a great Nation, in the name of *our* freedom and opportunity.

We had also landed on what would become the American shore as a people seeking religious and social freedom: liberty from religious persecution and social classification. But the formerly oppressed are easily intoxicated by new freedoms—being released from bondage without the inner restraints of practiced virtue they more readily mimic their former masters than renounce mastery. So, we imagined the myths of "manifest destiny" and "exceptionalism," mythologizing a simple lust for appropriation, a presumption of entitlement to the possessions of others; celebrating our freedom by destroying the freedom and lives of others; hiding the truth only from ourselves—that our self-described "exceptionalism" was the self-deception of a sinful soul; the sins of greed and vanity (The Christian seven deadly sins so well describe the selfish brain!).

One might wonder why the need to see ourselves as exceptional, what purpose in ascribing a privileged destiny to our actions other than the appearance of justification and the evasion of moral responsibility, assuring ourselves of our rightness? Consciousness of guilt precludes self-satisfaction, and so conscious guilt must be extinguished by self-righteousness. And what kind of mind needs pretense to obscure reality unless reality is damning? When Truth condemns, the lie is salvation—and "wokeness" the enemy. Such rationalization works only for those without conscience. A true conscience is independent of one's will; it is a brain function not silenced by the prefrontal's submission to the amygdala's emotional dictates. A raging conscience is the scream of the "better angel."

We must then forswear and overcome the selfish individualism that has forestalled the great promise of common liberty, knowing that our fight is not against America; that we must stand for the principles that gave birth to America, lest we also fail her. For America was never only a people, or a land. America is an idea that history has pursued through countless struggles, and the lives of so many known and unknown patriots, for the inalienable Rights of Man. The present generations of Americans have yet to carry that idea forward, because we are stuck in fear-driven competitions for individual security. And so, a whole people can fail their country. Yet there are those—"libertarian" conservatives—who say there is no "country," that there are only living individuals with private desires; no transcendent purposes that oblige a concession of selfish concerns; no preceding sacrifices that command us to honor and give obedience to something other than ourselves. It is an ideology of selfishness we suffer, by which we have taken the greatest of human endowments—the capacity for self-improvement—and made it lesser... made it an obsession for self-indulgence.

Yet fairness demands that living Americans not be condemned by the failures of past Americans. Only we must know that we do not descend from gods; and that there never was a manifest destiny, no exceptionalism, then, or now. *Truth and Justice give exemption to no time and no people*, we are what we do, no matter what we say or claim about ourselves. There will be no escaping historical judgment for what we ourselves stand for in the present. The moral errors of our predecessors do not condemn us, but ours will. **"Ye shall know them by their fruits."**

....

I have attempted to describe the primary elements of the fear-based hypothesis—the idea that a genetically hyper reactive amygdala drives brain development toward an aggressive selfishness that seeks economic and political dominion as a defense against its fears. It is the brain that pursues authoritarian rule in opposition to democracy's promise of human equality.

I have argued the economic and political consequences of the brain's formation to fear; the most significant being that the anti-social brain formation (cognitive brain in alliance with the amygdala's fear) suppresses empathic sensibility. When fear predominates over the incipient brain the potential for moral sensibility recedes, perhaps never to be reclaimed. What then emerges is the sociopathic personality.

And so, the dynamic of exerted insecurity, the fearful mind suffered to defend itself, unrestrained by moral conscience, underlies all aggressive and insistent pursuits of domination and superior possession, culturally acceptable and unacceptable, legal and illegal. The sociopath performs his compulsions according to his talents—and opportunities.

The tragic and summary conclusion is that this brain deficiency—the failure of the prefrontal cortex to supervise the amygdala is an evolutionarily regressive formation that is reinforced by the social arrangements of neoliberalism— the material reward of selfishness. We are not only stuck in our evolutionary development, we are pulling ourselves backwards, withdrawing from the possibility of further evolution—the ultimate sin against the gift of creation. The whole history of the human struggle for freedom has been a drama pitting the dream of liberty from regimes of control and domination. Humanity has allowed its capacity for reason to be captured away from integration with moral sensibility into a sociopathic obsession with superiority as the means to survival, leaving the better angel born yet unborn, conceived yet not released fully into life, a dream without wings, left only to wander a world without sky.

The ideas that make up the needed vision need not be derived from old or new doctrines. We need no external theories, no foreign beliefs. We have had for two and a half centuries in our own founding documents the most glorious and revolutionary thoughts ever written. Though forestalled,

America's founding principles of equal creation and inalienable rights are our guides.

As we learned from Thomas Paine, **"forms grow out of principles."** Our founding principles of **"created equal"** and **"unalienable rights"** have not dictated our economic forms; we do not do as our origin proclaimed.

So we must know our principles and embrace their implications: that the right to life requires the support of life; that the health of the natural environment is necessary to our survival, and its care a duty before creation; that our Nation's natural resources belong to all of its citizens; that corporate production should serve common wealth not private wealth—the charter of corporations as well as government should be for common purposes, not individual; that technology be viewed as a means for increasing the goods of general well-being; public financing of political campaigns; ending party identifications for political candidates so that all candidates, not just members of *private political monopolies*, can present their ideas to the electorate; increased transparency and oversight of governmental and corporate operations; national reaffirmation that the first purpose of government is the physical and economic security of all individuals; a major shifting of economic incentives and an application of wealth toward social infrastructure, from the fortresses of unjust privilege to socially indispensable programs such as national debt reduction, universal higher education, healthcare, and scientific research; and a program of early childhood education that accords with what neuroscience knows about *the developmental requirements of the infant brain*; the rehabilitation of the population's mental and physical health through less stress and anxiety; and perhaps most urgently, a world-wide treaty for the phased elimination of military establishments——so we can make plans for peace instead of war (The very existence of an army is a testament to human failure).

But the key to it all is security: protecting the human brain from the myriad debilitations of fear. This can be done through the emergence of Fundamental Democracy, where the economy is made for people, not people for the economy (To value human beings by market demand is to pay adults who play games with a ball $20 million a year while leaving millions of children imprisoned in poverty, unvalued by the larger community, uneducated, uninspired, and robbed of rightful prospects; trapped in environments that immediately dwarf their neurological possibilities; a beginning to life that constrains so many to unrealized lives. Such is a horrendous failure to uphold the natural rights of life.

It is not assumed here that such a transformation would be easy, only that it is essential. And I can imagine no greater adventure than the transformation of the destructive patterns of human history, formed out of fear and alterable by the environmental alleviation of fear. Yet, as we have seen throughout this text, change is among the amygdala's great fears. Nature gave us fear only that we might survive. But from the opening paragraph we see that survival is only the first step of evolution, that life exists to thrive and become, not to be devoured by fear. Thus, to evolve for the better we must live in an environment that supports what is better. So, the question is: can we agree to evolve beyond the reptilian brain? Will we embrace universal security as an implicit requirement of the inalienable right to life, or will we insist on the freedom of individual opportunity to continue the game of domination, one over the other? Human liberty will depend on the restraint of human freedom.

Arguments for truth are not in themselves political. They are not opposed to any person or community; they are opposed to falsehoods. Those who are defensive against the probing of Truth have found safety and benefit in falsehood. Truth is found through the archaeology of curiosity, guided by intuition; by a wondering mind not bound or limited by preconception. We find Truth in humility and in gratitude that we are privileged with the ability to wonder, the curiosity to explore, the vision to inspire effort... and the sensibility and courage to dissent from the harmful prescriptions of others. Yet we may never grasp the ultimate Truth directly, with our eye clearly upon it. We may only find intermediate Truths by eliminating one at a time the errors and falsehoods by which we have lived our lives; we may only find Truth through the failure and exhaustion of our certainties. But that is all that progress requires, that we always step beyond our failed certainties, that the journey to become never ends. Yet in giving our best we must know that the consequences that fate imposes give no consideration to our efforts or the intentions of goodwill. Success is never a promise; the effort made is our legacy. We have come from the past into the present. And the present is not long—only a moment rushing in from the future, falling instantly into the past. But it is only in this ever-moving, immeasurable moment that we have the freedom to choose. Our choice is between faith in the heart's compassion or the fears of the amygdala. Our choice will be our future; and it will be our children's future, until they rise and choose for themselves.

There is great talent in America, great scientific knowledge and technological capability. What is needed is an ideology of justice and a true freedom resting on a secured liberty of life, to replace the ideology of selfishness—a vision that offers a path to fulfillment as well as security. We have a duty to the past to advance what was given us. And we have a duty to the future to correct the course of the present. If we can change ourselves, if we can repent of our submission to the amygdala's fear and free ourselves from selfishness, we can pass unlimited promises to the future. But to express our freedom we must know that history and tradition are advisory, not prescriptive. The past must never be allowed to compel the present. The social forms made in the past were made for the past and do not bind us, except as we renew our allegiance. It is the self-evident Truths and principles of our founding as a Nation that must be our guide. And the human heart that first inspired those principles must be free to alter the forms and institutions that no longer serve them—or never served them!

"Let us re-adopt the Declaration of Independence, and with it, the practices, and policy, which harmonize with it." (Abraham Lincoln, Oct. 16, 1854).

Life is an exercise, like the repetitious lifting of a weight to build muscle. All thought and action are good or evil, useful or harmful, according to the life they build. It is not the sensation in the moment—the fun or pleasure or profit—that is the ultimate value of the thought or act, but the state of life and mind for which it is a practice toward becoming. To always seek the easy amusement or satisfaction or profit of the egocentric moment is often to forgo the efforts that build possibilities. When we practice selfishness, we stoke and prolong the reptilian nightmare within ourselves. If we would try friendship and compassion and mutual security, we would free the human brain from fear; and then we could build a place where dreams do come true. It would be a great people who did that for their children.

"The ultimate test of a moral society is the kind of world that it leaves to its children." (Dietrich Bonhoeffer).

It is important to state that this hypothesis intends to condemn no person or persons. We all begin life with a neural universe we have not chosen—we do not choose ourselves; no one is self-made. Nor do we choose the initial environments and experiences that so impact who we become. To be sure, as we mature, we come to "choose" the experiences which will further mold us. But at the beginning and throughout the earliest years of life we are made by everything but ourselves—our unique genetic compositions and our indoctrinating birth environments. "We" are not even here yet. The eventual sentient self-conscious "I" is waiting to be determined. But having not been self-made does not remove our responsibility to respect the lives of others, and to ever search for our better selves, waiting somewhere in our dreams of possibility.

But we cannot find possibility without first finding Truth. Is there a state of mind for which Truth is an enemy? Yes, a brain filled with fear relieving conceptions, for which Truth is danger pounding on the door—it is the brain of the book burner.

. . . .

As author, I recognize that an argument filled with so many repetitions will have been an annoyance to some readers. To them I apologize. But I cannot say it was unintended, for the purpose of repetition is to emphasize critical points, hopefully making them indelible. Also, the brain develops and functions by establishing belief and behavior patterns—early life experience and indoctrinations that connect our neurons into circuits of habit and conformity—conditioned and reinforced by repetition. Thus, it requires new repetitions to modify or extinguish old repetitions—that, after all, is what behavior and cognitive modification theory is about—*wearing down the mental content we were given, and replacing it with a mind of our own*. The greatest freedom is in making ourselves. (And as every old carpenter knows, the harder the wood the more hammering the nail requires).

And so, my concern, as it must be for anyone presuming to address the public mind, was to try to keep the pieces of the argument, and the connections between the pieces clear for all readers. My judgment was that the hypothesis and its intertwining elements required recurring summaries and reminders; necessary to the goal of understanding, always a prerequisite to the goal of persuasion. If these thoughts are true, then I simply say that Truth cannot be too often repeated. If they are not true, then I have only succeeded in conceiving falsehoods, in which case I hope the reader has somehow gained wisdom in discovering them so.

Finally, by appeal to personal privilege I grant myself these last repetitions:

The search for Truth requires a reach that sometimes finds mistake, but the reach is imperative, for we must know the Truth or live by lies and falsehoods. And to accept the lie is to sacrifice the dream.

Whither is fled the visionary gleam?
Where is it now, the glory and the dream?
(William Wordsworth, *Ode on Intimations...*)

Community salvation will require the heart of the whole people to find a common voice, and speak their own prophesy for the renewal of democracy, and the resurrection of the better angel. It should begin in America, where the cry for common liberty was raised by a common man—common in his beginnings, foremost in his destiny.

"We have it in our power to begin the world over again." (Thomas Paine; *Common Sense*, Philadelphia, January 1776).

"Without the pen of the author of *Common Sense*, the sword of Washington would have been raised in vain." (John Adams)

Mr. Adams was not an admirer of Thomas Paine; yet he could not keep from acknowledging his contribution to America's Independence. Grudging praise is perhaps the greatest praise, for it means Reason's acknowledgement has overcome Emotion's reluctance.

Epilogue

This effort is dedicated to all those who have hearts mightier than their egos, and who have personally experienced that giving is the greatest gift we can give to ourselves; and offered with patience to all those who are discomforted by the implications of America's founding principles.

A hypothesis is not a proclamation. It is a proposition composed of stated principles, apparent facts and logical inferences, subject to confirmation and refutation. Among creatures so capable of fallacy only Truth can have the final word, however delayed its arrival. *For Man is not the measure of Truth; it is He who is measured.*

The pervading purpose of this hypothesis has been to understand the reactionary conservative brain: what it is and why it is... why its resistance to human equality, why its moral indifference to unfairness, its inattention to the mental disruption of disadvantaged children, why its greed for social privilege, why its preference for mystical beliefs over scientific facts? And why its hate for a government whose purpose is to secure the inalienable rights of life? The argument here is the conservative brain is more extreme in its intents because it is compelled by the emotions of threat to its survival. Liberality, seeking change in the name of progress and justice looks to the conservative amygdala like an attack of the body snatchers; hence the demonizing of "liberals" and "do-gooders" and "bleeding hearts." Condemning liberals for their allegiance to ethical principles and compassion for others is for the conservative brain an unwitting act of confession.

The criticism of conservative psychology is not a criticism of what is considered conservative philosophy—the upholding of values and principles, and respect for the cautions of prudence—*except as those values and principles presume to justify and preserve the unjust accomplishments of the past.*

The human brain remains a largely unknown universe. The implications of the Democracy Covenant are not. And the cause could not be higher: humanity needs a future that does not mirror its past. Which means, overcoming the reptilian brain.

....

This author is forever humbled before the giants of human thought by whom he is gratefully inspired. High among them is Thomas Paine, author of *Common Sense*, the book that energized public support for American Independence; and the larger cause for the rights of common humanity. Paine was an Englishman newcomer to America, arriving in 1774. *Common Sense* was first published anonymously in January 1776, six months before The Declaration. The pamphlet was purchased by 20% of the colonial population in 1776. In contemporary America's population that is equivalent to 66 million copies! When it was inquired who the author was, he wrote this:

"Who the Author of this Production is, is wholly unnecessary to the Public, as the Object for Attention is

the Doctrine itself, not the Man. Yet it may not be unnecessary to say, That he is unconnected with any Party, and under no sort of Influence public or private, but the influence of reason and principle." (Philadelphia, February 14, 1776).

The focus on messengers aids in the avoidance of messages. *No idea was ever true, or false, because of who said it.*

(Thomas Paine donated the royalties from *Common Sense* to George Washington's Continental Army).

As is the case with all explorations for Truth, to be continued...

Truth and Justice
Are the Chrysalis;
Love and Liberty,
The Butterfly.

Percivis